MEMORIES OF JOHN GALSWORTHY

MEMORIES OF
JOHN GALSWORTHY

By His Sister
M. E. REYNOLDS

New York
FREDERICK A. STOKES COMPANY
Publishers

To
HIS MEMORY

AUTHOR'S NOTE

ALTHOUGH this little memoir gives a slight outline of my brother's life, it lays no claim to be called a 'biography' in the usual sense of the word. I have merely tried to record my personal impression of his character, as briefly and simply as possible.

Part of my account of the early days—written several years ago—has been quoted by Mr. H. V. Marrot in his *Life and Letters of John Galsworthy*.

The miscellaneous collection of letters following the memoir has been selected with only one object in view: that of illustrating points of character indicated in the memoir itself. My thanks are due to the recipients of these letters, and to my brother's literary Executor, for permitting their publication.

LIST OF ILLUSTRATIONS

LIST OF ILLUSTRATIONS

FACING PAGE

J. G. AND HIS WIFE, ADA . . *Frontispiece*

J. G.'S FATHER AND MOTHER 13

LATER PORTRAITS OF J. G.'S PARENTS . . . 15

THE FOUR CHILDREN 16

LATER PORTRAITS OF THE FOUR CHILDREN . . 21

LILIAN AND HER HUSBAND, PROF. GEORG SAUTER 22

HUBERT AND HIS WIFE, LINA 28

MABEL AND HER HUSBAND, T. B. REYNOLDS . . 30

J. G. IN 1911 32

ADA GALSWORTHY, NÉE COOPER 34

IN THE STUDY, BURY HOUSE 37

IN THE PORCH, BURY HOUSE 40

THE STUDY WINDOW, GROVE LODGE . . . 52

M. E. R. AND VERONICA 66

LILIAN WITH HER SON, RUDOLF 70

J. G. WITH OWEN, VERONICA AND "CHRIS" . . 70

J. G. RIDING AT WINGSTONE 83

A. G. WITH H. W. NEVINSON AND JOHN MASEFIELD . 104

VERONICA REYNOLDS IN RAGLAN CASTLE . . 111

J. G. BOUND FOR AMERICA, 1925 . . . 115

J. G. AND HIS WIFE IN ARIZONA 116

J. G. IN 1927 120

J. G.'S GODSON, OWEN BLAIR REYNOLDS . . 123

ADA GALSWORTHY IN 1929 124

J. G. IN 1928 128

PART I

BLANCHE BAILEY GALSWORTHY
née Bartleet
1837-1915

JOHN GALSWORTHY, SENR.
"Old Jolyon"
1817-1904

B. B. G. AND HER SON,
JOHN

MY brother John Galsworthy was born on the 14th of August, 1867, in a house called 'Parkfield', on the high road between Kingston Vale and Kingston Hill in Surrey.

He left that house when only a few months old, and had, of course, no recollection of it. But there it stands to this day, outwardly, at any rate, unaltered since the time when our father, John Galsworthy senior, moved into it, with his wife and their little three-year-old daughter, Blanche Lilian, from his house in Portland Place.

Our father was a keen, though undemonstrative lover of nature, delighting in anything which could be called a 'view'. On the edge of Coombe Warren, a vacant stretch of land on the top of Kingston Hill, he had discovered a site after his own heart, with a view extending to the Epsom Downs, and even, on fine days, to Leith Hill. There he built, on plots practically adjoining each other, first one, then a second, and finally a third house, on the south side of the Warren, taking a short lease of 'Parkfield' in the meanwhile, that he might be near enough in his spare time to keep an eye on the work whilst the first of the three houses was going up.

That house—called in those days simply 'Coombe Warren', being the very first to be built on that land—was, as it were, the Big Bear of the trio. In it my younger brother

Hubert and I were born, in 1869 and 1871, respectively. On its right was built the second house, or Middle Bear, called at that time 'Coombe Leigh', and on its left the Little Bear, 'Coombe Croft'.

In these three houses our father lived with his family for seventeen years, occupying or letting first one and then the other, as the spirit moved him.

There is no doubt that in wording his picture of 'Robin Hill' in the *Forsyte Saga* my brother had the site and grounds of ' Coombe Warren ' in his mind. But not one of those three houses built by my father—the first of which was completely demolished some years ago—bore the slightest resemblance to the house of 'Robin Hill'.

As I was only three years old when we moved into Coombe Leigh, I can remember but little of our life in the first house, Coombe Warren, and nothing at all of my brother in connection with it. But it is easy to form an idea of his childhood, for although several details are distinctly different, the picture he has drawn in the sketch called *Awakening* of the little boy Jon's early life is practically a description of his own.

The chief point of non-resemblance lies in the personalities of the parents. Neither our father nor our mother bore any likeness whatever to the parents of little Jon.

It is in the older Jolyon of *The Man of Property* and the *Indian Summer* that we find many a trait of our father skilfully reproduced ; and the sketch in *A Motley* (first edition) called *A Portrait* is a

J. G. SENR.

B.B.G.

J. G. SENR.

study of him so touching, understanding and complete as to cause wonder that even his own son, at a comparatively early age, should have possessed the degree of insight and sympathy necessary to its achievement.

Here I should like to say that, to my mind, apart from the one acknowledged instance of Old Jolyon, too much has been made of the supposed likeness to real persons of the 'Forsyte' family in general. My brother did indeed observe and adapt many typical characteristics and idiosyncrasies of his relations, but in every case the individual underwent such drastic alteration at his hands that to label any one person in the 'Saga' as definitely 'taken' from any one relative in real life is to give a false impression.

.   .   .   .   .

The difference in age between our parents was twenty years, but even so *both* were grey-haired before most of us were born. Our earliest recollection of our father, therefore, was that of an elderly man, splendidly upright and sturdy, but with the silvery hair and the square, grey (later on snow-white), beard of the portrait on the opposite page.

Head of a firm of solicitors in Old Jewry, he went regularly to the City every morning at eleven, returning every evening at five. The leisurely keeping of these unexacting hours left him ample time, in addition to his Saturdays and Sundays, for the enjoyment of his home-life, his gardens and his 'views' to his heart's content; and my

memory of him in those happy days at Coombe is
that of one whose heart's content was a genial
thing, extracting the maximum of enjoyment and
the minimum of worry from all the good things
with which his own sane brain and a kindly lot
had endowed him.

Every fine evening, with a small child's hand
in his, he would make his careful rounds of the
stables, gardens, paddocks and little farmyard,
stroking the horses and cows, watching the
chickens and baby pigs, peering into the bushes
for the latest birds' nests—all with a pleasure
and eagerness as young and keen as that of the
child by his side. He had a special affection for
the three lovely Alderney cows, and liked to see
them grazing in the large paddock, right in the
middle of the garden.

No recollection of the early years at Coombe is
so vivid as that of those daily rounds with Father,
or the excitement of driving the 'T-cart' to and
from the station, to take him or fetch him home;
with Johnnie's roan cob pulling hard at the
reins, and portly old Haddon, the coachman,
sitting beside one. What a shapely beauty that
little cob was! and how nearly he cut short
Master Johnnie's career by running away with
him in Richmond Park and trying to scrape
him off against the trees there!

Our mother, too, we remember best very much
as she appears in the portrait here reproduced—
dainty and delicate, like a 'French Marquise', as
a friend once remarked while in act of painting
her miniature.

BLANCHE LILIAN
1864-1924

JOHN
1867-1933

HUBERT
B. 1869

MABEL EDITH
B. 1871

In the Coombe days she never was very strong. I remember her as constantly on the sofa, a piece of black Spanish lace over her head. Gentle and loving, devoted to her husband and children, and the "kindest mistress in the world", (to quote a dear old member of the staff, who always loved to talk of her), our mother, nevertheless, is not so prominent nor every-day a figure as our father in the hazy memory of those early days. With a staff of some fourteen souls to help or hinder her in the running of her children, her house and her grounds, it is perhaps small wonder if we saw her chiefly at certain fixed hours, or when we were 'naughty' or ill.

Of our elder sister, Lilian, I remember that even at that time she was so quiet and studious as to seem more than her three years older than John. A rare spirit in a frail body, it was she who brought to us three younger ones the greater part of such mental stimulus as our very normal, ordinary lives ever knew. Always quietly busy herself with her painting, reading, needlework or writing, it was she who would start interesting subjects for discussion; she who told us stories when we were little; she who opened our eyes and minds to beautiful things to be seen or heard or read.

.   .   .   .   .

'Johnnie' was taught at home, as we all were, by a series of governesses, English and foreign, until he was nine years old, when he was sent to a small preparatory school at Bournemouth, called 'Saugeen' and kept by Dr. and Mrs. Brackenbury.

B

There he was joined later by my brother Hubert and two or three cousins.

This led to several visits to Bournemouth by the rest of the family. In those days it was a pleasant place of unspoilt sands and pinewoods and clean bright sea. How vividly I remember to this day the hot Sunday scent of the pines on the edge of the cliff on the way to the little church, St. Swithin's, where Johnnie, with other little Saugeen boys, would be singing in the choir! And the delight of digging, with brothers and cousins, in the gold and silver sands of cliffs and beach, on those glorious days of real old-fashioned summer!

But the pictures stored in my poor memory of Johnnie's boyhood are woefully few and vague. For I was four years his junior, and he was mostly away at school, or staying with friends.

The general impression left is that of a normal, not at all unusual kind of boy. I know that he was healthy and active, good at games and school sports—as a number of cups and other trophies can testify; captain (in due course) of 'footer' and 'gym' at Harrow; a bad cricketer, but good tennis-player, horseman and shot.

He read voraciously, at an early age, all sorts of books of adventure, travel and history, and made himself short-sighted by generally doing this face downwards on the floor. The battles, naval and military, about which he read were worked out afterwards by means of all a boy's usual paraphernalia: lead-soldiers, spring-cannon, boats, bricks, etc. I can see him now, prone on the floor, or bending over the large round table in the nursery at 'The Leigh' or the schoolroom table at 'Coombe Croft', juggling his forces with busy hands and a sort of deadly earnestness, muttering commands about this or that, building a fort one moment, and knocking it down the next.

Great tournaments took place, too, upon the lawns, where he would lie, heels in air, in the sun that he so loved all his life long—smiting the busby-like heads of plantain-stalks one against the other, till only one 'conqueror', named after one of his favourite Arthurian or other heroes, would be left, a limp and sorry sight, to tell the tale. And the delicious string of names with which he ceremoniously christened our rotund, tabby tom-cat: "Puck, Pat-paw, Wilfred, Oeuf, Coeur-de-Chat, von Galsworthy" spoke eloquently of the exciting medley of matter seething in an imaginative small boy's mind!

He was our chief in all the wild games we played about the house and grounds on holidays; captain of the pillow-fights, and of the ships we built of beds and chests of drawers, with curtains and window-blinds rigged up for sails; leader of fierce raids on 'the enemy' (usually some long-suffering member of the staff), armed with cata-pults and water-squirts. But whereas the energy displayed by all on these occasions often ended in accidental damage to one or other of us, and consequent tantrums or tears from Hubert or me, I can remember no fits of temper on the part of Johnnie himself. Though willing enough to profit by our 'fagging', his rule was mild and his teasing good-humoured, and he never cared to bully his young brother.

I well remember the fierce billiard contests between the two boys, for they would get me to mark for them; and the exciting tennis-matches—'singles', on the courts on the lawn at 'The Leigh'—which I would watch from my favourite seat in the swing that hung from 'Old Jolyon's' oak near by. Very well matched they were, for Hubert, though two years younger, was the quicker and more 'wiry'—as also the quicker-tempered—of the two. John, as we were then beginning to call him, was a good loser. He played with more impersonality, and under a beating remained always master of himself.

At Harrow he went steadily up the school, being high in the Upper Sixth before he left. The music, there, was in the hands of John Farmer in those days, and between his influence and that of Mrs. Hutton, his house-master's enthusiastically musical wife, John developed a keenness for singing, of a kind, and became one of 'the Twelve'. I still have a folio full of the old British songs he used to sing: 'The Vicar of Bray', 'Ode to Tobacco', 'Songs of Araby', 'To Anthea', 'Lyrics' by Harold Boulton, Maude Valerie White and others; and the Harrow School Songs, of course! And I remember his mother's pride in a letter from John Farmer saying: "Your son is one of my rocks." His voice was not strong, but a light, pleasant baritone, no trace remaining of the tendency to flatness that had been notice-able when a treble at Saugeen.

LILIAN

JOHN

HUBERT

MABEL

He was Head of Mr. Hutton's house ('Moreton's') at the time when his young brother entered it. The latter became his tea-fag, and remembers to this day the musical resonance of Jack's call—the traditional call of 'Boy!'—that would summon him to his duties in the study. A friendly understanding, compounded of help with the junior's school-work, and liberty to 'pinch' portions of any cake already cut, seems to have obtained between the two!

In 1886 John left Harrow, and we all went down for his last Speech Day. About this time he went through the phase of dandyism peculiar to boys of his age, and I remember how we laughed that day to see 'Galer', as they called him, seated in state in the front row on the platform of 'Speecher', carefully flicking with his handkerchief at the dust on his patent-leather shoes!

His dress was always correct and careful, and he had a way of screwing the monocle acquired later, at Oxford, into his eye with a look of quizzical criticism which could reduce anyone's self-importance to its very lowest ebb.

And yet, he was so unassuming, so dear and void of actual conceit, that no-one would ever have dreamt of suggesting that 'Galer' was a 'puppy' or a prig.

The streak of dandyism, natural enough in one who was born and bred a 'Forsyte', faded gradually to a normal degree of respect for outward appearances, and in course of time the monocle, like his spectacles, was only used when really necessary, to correct the defective sight of the right eye. But the occasional quizzical expression, best, perhaps, described as the 'eye-glass attitude', survived into much later days, combining at times with a delicately caustic twist of speech to make its object thoroughly uncomfortable. If he disapproved of someone's views or conduct, the hints given of such disapproval, although reserved and sparing, were apt lightly to scathe the feelings of the person concerned. A sense of this danger accounted, I think, for the awe in which some folk held him.

.   .   .   .   .

The removal of the family to London took place in the spring of 1887, chiefly in order that Lily might be within reach of the lectures and concerts she wanted to attend.

After a year or two spent in a flat in Kensington, our father moved into one of the houses he owned in Cambridge Gate, Regent's Park. There he and our mother remained until after the marriage of Lilian in 1894 and of myself in 1897.

In the meantime John had entered New College, Oxford. There he again did well, and when the time came to take his degree in Law he just missed a 'First' by a narrow shave, being bracketed top of the 'Seconds' with another man.

He was quietly, if not conspicuously, popular at New College, and the two Commemorations

Lilian and her Husband, Prof. Georg Sauter

for which we went up were delightful experiences.

So far he had shewn no particularly strong bent or taste of any kind.

On coming down he took the lead suggested by our solicitor-father's connection with the Law, and started to read for the Bar. He went into chambers, and in due course 'ate' his 'dinners'. But his heart was never in the work, and when circumstances led him to drop it, while still in a briefless condition, I am sure he did so without regret.

In 1891 our father, being chairman of the company, sent both John and Hubert on an expedition to Nanaimo, Vancouver Island, British Columbia, ostensibly to inquire into the affairs of a coal-mine in that district, but incidentally for the sake of the experience and pleasure of the trip. A letter to myself tells of camping, fishing and shooting, with but poor luck; of narrow escapes from being lost in the forests and drowned in one of the lakes. The latter adventure Hubert afterwards retailed with glee and unction. "Old Jack bobbed up to the surface again in an upright position and looking as cool as a cucumber," he said, "with his rod still in his hands, and his eye-glass still in his eye! You never saw anything quite so funny!" Luckily, in those days the hair on the top of his head, later so conspicuous by its absence, was fairly thick and strong. Hubert took a hearty grab at it, and helped him back to safety on the raft.

Messages to Father in one of John's letters indicate, however, that the main object of the journey was not neglected. It ends with a friendly jibe at the rest of the family, spending their summer holidays at Bayreuth, for their sudden conversion to Wagner—a composer for whose work my brother was never able to cultivate any affection, in spite of all efforts on the part of his friend Alec Tassell (a great enthusiast) to rope him, with the rest of us, into the fold.

His favourite music in after life was: Bach, notably the Brandenburg and other concertos, which he was careful not to miss—especially if Myra Hess were the pianiste—when they were done at the 'Proms'; Brahms, including numbers of the songs; nearly all Chopin; the César Franck piano and violin sonata; Gluck's 'Orfeo'; Bizet's 'Carmen'; 'The Beggar's Opera'; 'Tales of Hoffmann'; folk-music of all nations: British (including the Kennedy-Fraser collections of Hebridean songs), Old French, Pyrenean, Spanish, Hungarian, Styrian, and so on. Schumann, for some reason, he never cared for, and if his wife ever started to play one of his works, an emphatic "No!" from the arm-chair would indicate that the right note had not been struck!

·   ·   ·   ·   ·

On the boys' return from America, John took to studying Admiralty Law and Navigation.

A first young love affair failed to end happily, and a stage of blank depression set in.

Then our father, who always felt any trouble

of his children acutely, suggested the diversion of a long sea voyage, and, in company with his old Harrow friend E. L. Sanderson, Jack sailed in November 1892, in the P. & O. S.S. *Oruba*, on a tour to the Fiji Islands, Ceylon, New Zealand and Australia.

Some letters to Lilian and myself, written from the boat, from Australia, and from Tavini, shew a growing observation of beauty in scenery, and a sympathetic interest in some of his travelling-companions; but there is nothing particularly striking about them in either matter or style.

The return voyage of six months was made in the sailing-ship *Torrens*, as far as the Cape.

Jack wrote that he passed much of the time in learning practical navigation.

It was on this return voyage in the *Torrens* that he and Ted Sanderson made the acquaintance of Joseph Conrad, who was first mate of that ship at the time.

Although not much seems to have passed between the three during that voyage concerning Conrad's own first literary effort *Almayer's Folly*, which he had not yet summoned conviction enough to offer to any publisher, there can be no doubt that it was the contact with his acutely observant, introspective type of brain and vivid speech which gave my brother's own mind its first push towards the appreciation of literature; although it remained for Ada Cooper to make the suggestion that actually induced him to try his own hand, and he often declared that but for her he never would have done so.

The friendship begun at sea was continued on land. Ted Sanderson's home, the delightful old Schoolhouse of Elstree, became Jack's constant resort. Conrad also frequently spent a few days there, and many stimulating discussions took place.

I stayed there often myself, and I remember that both Ted and his mother—'Mrs. Kitty', as everyone called her—took a hand, and considerable trouble, in editing the already amazingly excellent English of their Polish friend's 'Almayer' manuscript, and in generally screwing up Conrad's courage to the sticking-point of publication.

The warmth of the latter's friendship for the house of Sanderson is clearly shewn in letters published by Mr. Jean-Aubry in his book: *The Life and Letters of Joseph Conrad.*

My brother and I were equally devoted to the family. Jack, indeed, for several years, spent so much of his time there that I feel that some little description of Elstree and its inhabitants of that time is hardly out of place.

The father, Lancelot Sanderson, Headmaster of the School, was absorbed in his work, and delicate in health. We saw but little of him. His wife, 'Mrs. Kitty', mother of sixteen children, but still young as any of her daughters in their teens, was a truly amazing woman. Whether she actually came of an Irish family or not I have no idea, but to call her 'Irish' is perhaps the best way to indicate the delightful, generous warmth of her vital personality, her charmingly irresponsible

ways, and her cheerful, birdlike chatting, with
its ultra-affectionate expressions and head poised
a little to one side.

They sat down, habitually, in their private
dining-room, some twelve to fifteen persons to a
meal—with a nurseryful of youngsters upstairs—
but there was always food, and a bed to follow,
for any of the friends, expected or unexpected,
who were 'dropping in' all the time; though the
bed might be a hard one, creaky and lumpy, in
some little bare room with a queer name in any
god-forsaken part of that capacious, rambling
old house.

Hospitality, of a rather baffling kind, was the
order of every day. Everyone was welcome, but
—perhaps for that very reason—all were usually
left in the most casual way to amuse and look
after themselves.

So picturesque a crowd as the thirteen children
surviving at that time we shall certainly never
see again: half of them fair, with very light hair;
most of the rest with hair that was nearly black;
some of them strikingly handsome, and not one
really plain one amongst the lot!

They all loved Jack. With the elder ones he
struck up several friendships, and his patience with
the little ones who swarmed over him all day
long was a pleasant thing to see.

His very first 'work' was, I think, a delightful
little play that he planned for a number of the
smallest ones to act with him on the schoolhouse
stage. Even the baby-girl of three had her tiny
part, and got through it, with as much credit to

his tactful 'management' as to her own small self.

Acting had been a hobby of Jack's for several years before this. He was a member of the 'O.U.D.S.' of Oxford; and for the private theatricals of vacation-time both his acting and his management were often in request.

.   .   .   .   .

Two or three years before we left Coombe for London our father had started an annual custom of renting a country house, with shooting and fishing, for the eight or nine weeks of the boys' summer holidays.

In 1883 and 1884 he took a house called Whyddon Park, about eight miles from Chagford, and gave us our first taste of real wild country and his native Devon.

That simple grey stone house stood in a glorious wilderness of rough tor-side, of pine-trees, boulders, bracken and amber-coloured streams—a paradise for two healthy boys with guns and rods in quest of the homely bunny and elusive trout, and for an untirable small girl careering wildly about in a gay cotton sun-bonnet.

There for the first time I realised our father's great love for beauty in nature; and our mutual delight in the sunsets on the moors remains a golden memory.

My mother had a fine gift of hospitality. She took a special pleasure in planning her lists of guests so as to form the most congenial combinations, and her house-parties and dances were

Hubert and his Wife, Lina, née Orfila

always highly appreciated. In fact, both our parents had a talent for promoting enjoyment, and gave their children year after year a splendid time.

Jack was a staunch friend, and kept up with several of his Harrow and Oxford pals for many years. Amongst the names of those with whom he was most intimate, some of whom came to stay with us summer after summer, the following occur to me most readily:

C. J. E. Parker, C. S. Vaughan (and his sister Margaret), St. John Hornby and his brother, J. W. Hills, George Harris, J. St. F. Fair (whose sister Gertrude, Mrs. E. M. Butler, was my first school-friend), Charles Hill (and his sisters), Guy Granet, Claud Douglas Pennant, Miles Davies (and his sister Lilian), G. Bromley-Martin, Alec Tassell, and two cousins, Frank Easton and Herbert Marshall (and their wives, Grace and Olga).

For several summers we went to moors in Scotland, with occasional visits (without the boys) to Switzerland, Bavaria or the Tirol, in between. Then back to Devon, to the rectories of Lydford and Hayford, always with shooting on the neighbouring moors. And during the many visits paid by Jack to the country houses of his friends shooting always formed the chief attraction. But though to his normal British love of any trial of skill the fascination of the sport was irresistible, to his sensitive humanity the attending tragedies to bird and beast were always a horror, from the first.

It took some ten years before he finally 'had it out' with himself on this point. But one season the definite thing happened inside him, and Jack never shot nor hunted again.

Some years later he wrote the poignant little sketch called: *Reverie of a Sportsman* (in the first *Sheaf*), in which the reproachful shades of all his victims pass judgment on the 'Brute'.

In a hundred other ways he served the cause of the humane treatment of animals during the latter part of his life—by appeals and subscriptions, in books and plays, in lectures and articles, and, above all, by his painful personal investigations and reports.

It was in 1912, I think, that he made a tour of slaughter-houses in England and wrote a report exposing the inhumanity of the customary system, with the object—partially successful—of getting the 'Humane Killer' generally adopted.

To a man whose sympathy for animals had reached so acute a pitch this tour of inspection must have been an agonising experience.

.　　.　　.　　.　　.

It was 1895, and he was twenty-eight, before my brother started to 'write'; and then the first little book of short stories *From the Four Winds* was issued tentatively, under the nom-de-plume 'John Sinjohn' ('John the Son of John').

I well remember his bringing the MS. to the morning-room at Cambridge Gate, where we girls worked and practised, with a plea for help on punctuation, which was not his strong point at the time.

The book was kindly, though not brilliantly

MABEL AND HER HUSBAND, THOMAS BLAIR REYNOLDS

received, as were the next three volumes: *Jocelyn*, *Villa Rubein*, and *A Man of Devon*; and on the appearance of his fifth book, *The Island Pharisees*, the pseudonym was discarded.

That book, *The Island Pharisees*, contains many passages and characters that savour strongly (to one who shared them with him) of the old Elstree days, with their half-satisfying experiences and incomplete friendships; and in nearly all those early books may be sensed a wistful reaching out towards an ideal personal relationship as yet unrealised.

Our parents were both rather reserved and undemonstrative, and my personal impression is that John's abandonment of the Law for the probably unlucrative profession of a writer was received by them in a quiet and tactful manner that did credit to their self-control. For no 'Forsyte' could be expected to *welcome* such a change. To any Forsyte the question whether his son was likely to 'make money' or not would bring a pang of anxiety, or, if capable of answer in the affirmative, an unconscious, involuntary increase of respect. If you were 'successful' you 'made money'. If you did not make money—no matter what the quality of your work—you were not a success; more because you had, as it were, failed to stamp your achievement with the accepted hall-mark, than because any undue value was placed on wealth for its own sake. That our father forbore to worry Jack on the score of his desertion of a profession in which, given his finely-tempered, logical brain and his ready-made

legal connection, there was every likelihood of
his making good, shewed, therefore, a degree of
tolerant and affectionate understanding beyond
what might justly have been expected.

Up to that time no Galsworthy had, to our
knowledge, been an artist of any serious inten-
tion, literary or otherwise. It must have been
inconceivable to our parents that John's literary
achievements would ever really justify his apostasy.
Yet they watched his early efforts with pride, and
a certain characteristic serenity and optimism—
regarding it all, perhaps, as an interesting hobby
for a young man!

It is a grief that our father did not live to know
how fully that tentative confidence was to be
justified. His death, in 1904, occurred two years
before the appearance of *The Man of Property*;
that of our mother not till 1915, just before the
Little Man Satires and *The Freelands*. During the
intervening eleven years John had published so
much fine work that his mother, at least, had the
satisfaction of knowing that he had 'found himself' and stood already high in the estimation of
colleagues and public.

In his tenderly-conceived creations Frances
Freeland and the *Grey Angel*, and in a trait here
and there of Margery Pendyce, my brother has
recorded his impressions of our mother's character with a truth and sensitiveness of touch
remarkable in one of the opposite sex; especially
in view of the fact that a young man in normal
circumstances, passing from 'Prep-School' to
Public School, then to the Varsity, and finally

J. G.

1911

[Photo by E. O. Hoppé]

to independent life in rooms of his own, and marriage, does not see very much of his parents.

An exaggerated impression may have been given elsewhere concerning "want of sympathy between J. G. and his mother". This, such as it was, lay rather in superficial than in significant matters; in points of taste and opinion rather than of character; and perhaps, most of all, in the skin-deep friction so often existing between members of different generations. Under the natural irritation caused by her tendency to over-solicitude, and by her—occasionally—almost prudish, 'early Victorian' admonitions, lay a deep and understanding reverence on his part for her really great qualities, of unselfish devotion and endurance.

The same tender insight which informed the portraiture of his mother permeated all his attitude towards women, in real life as well as in his work.

In his very first book *From the Four Winds* there is a short tale already illustrating his passionately chivalrous feeling towards womanhood in any state of oppression or distress, and his loathing of that type of male mentality which extends the sense of property to its womenkind. And hardly a book or play that followed but has dealt, more or less poignantly, in one form or another, with the same theme.

It must be obvious to all that such a preoccupation—so intense as to amount almost to an obsession—must have had its roots in personal

c

experience of some kind, and this was indeed, the fact.

It was one of life's most amazingly-contrived misfits that Ada Cooper's unhappy marriage with a cousin of our own should have taken place only a few weeks before we met her.

I remember well the great impression left on us all, at a dinner given in their honour, by the rare, dark, dainty beauty of the bride. A mutual passion for music soon led to frequent meetings between her and myself, and the supreme friendship that arose between her and my brother also found opportunity to develop with lightning speed.

Before long her married life came to an untimely end. She left her husband, and came to live, near our house on Campden Hill, alone. For twelve years (from first to last) she and my brother waited for each other, rather than bring to our dear old father, in his last ailing years, the public scandal of a divorce, which he, with his Victorian traditions, would have felt as a deep disgrace.

Then came his death, in 1904; the proceedings followed as soon as possible, and they were married, at last.

.   .   .   .   .

For some years John and his wife divided their time between a London life in their house in Addison Road, peaceful sojourns at Wingstone, Manaton—the Devon farm which had known them well in the past—and travel.

Then they gave up the house in Addison Road,

ADA GALSWORTHY, NÉE COOPER

stayed for five years—1913 to 1918—in a flat in Adelphi Terrace House, and finally moved into the old-world 'Grove Lodge', a stone's throw from the Heath, at Hampstead.

Here they lived, during the warmer months, for many years, faithfully tended always by the same devoted staff of three competent servants.

Their occupations during the War were characteristically unostentatious. His were mostly confined to writing useful articles and appeals, contributing largely to innumerable funds, and generally helping where he could.

But in 1916 he decided to learn massage, and took his skill, as soon as acquired, to a war-hospital in the south-east of France, where they both worked for about five months—he treating wounded 'poilus', where treatment by massage was indicated, and she acting in charge of the linen, clothing, correspondence and other departments. Here their considerable knowledge of French and 'penchant' for French people stood them in good stead.

My brother had a hand with a particularly comforting touch, warm, firm, and gentle, and I was not surprised by a sentence in one of his letters which ran as follows:

"My massage seems, oddly enough, to be of some use."

. . . . . .

In October, 1924 our sister Lilian died, to the great grief of us all.

The internment and subsequent repatriation of her Bavarian husband, Prof. Georg Sauter, during

the War, and the internment of her son Rudolf
in Alexandra Palace, had broken her always frail
health, and sapped her powers of resistance. The
end came quickly as the blowing out of a flame.

My brother's untiring care and sympathy had
never failed her, and, now that she was gone, he
and his wife, having no children of their own,
suggested that Rudolf (her only child) and his
wife Viola should make their home with them.

That winter's health-tour in North Africa prov-
ing the harmonious working of the combination,
my sister's house at Hendon was sold on their
return, and the quartet set out to find a country
house, to serve as permanent home for the younger
and pied-à-terre for the elder couple.

By the autumn of 1926 they had found and
bought a property called 'Bury House', close to
the Sussex Downs, in the neighbourhood of
Amberley, Arundel and Pulborough.

Here, during the six years which remained to
him of life, 'J. G.' found full scope for his paternal
and patriarchal instincts—building model cot-
tages for those who served him, and a bungalow
for the district nurse; levelling a cricket-field for
the recreation of villagers and staff; and living,
generally, a healthy country life, with his family,
his horses, and his dogs.

He was much attached to Lilian's artist son,
and took the liveliest interest in his work (as in
that of my own son, Owen—also a painter, and
his godson); and the addition of the younger
couple to his household proved a great enrichment
of life.

IN THE STUDY, BURY HOUSE

[Photo by London General Press]

A glance over the wide range of J. G.'s literary work would lead one to suppose that the whole of his time must have gone to the making of it—to the exclusion of any ordinary social existence. The fact that this was by no means the case is a proof that the inspiration of the artist need not be a wanton thing, of unregulated caprice, requiring to be nursed and fostered in abnormal conditions, but may be a deep, reliable well of subconscious creative faculty, responding the more faithfully to demand as the will of the artist becomes trained to regularity of effort.

The self-control which restrained him from weak exhibitions of temper as a boy, and led him to continue exercise of all kinds in after life in order to keep himself 'fit', developed into a settled mastery of all his powers and impulses, which enabled him to reduce what might well have become a hopeless chaos of conflicting claims to an ordered course of continuous mental and physical activity.

The daily programme of his home life was of an amazing sanity, and quietly packed with an incredible number of unobtrusive doings. At the country house it took shape mostly as follows:

A ride on the Downs before breakfast, rain or shine, accompanied by his nephew and the dogs; breakfast to the tune of the copious early mail, followed by swift and drastic dealing with that mail, in the study, with the help of his wife. Then, two or three hours of solid undisturbed creative work—sitting, on any fine day, in a sunny, sheltered bay of the terrace, with block on knee and a dog or two at his feet.

After lunch, in fine weather, there would be a walk with the dogs, tennis, or a drive, or calls exchanged with friends. Tea was followed usually by light literary work, revising, and so on; sometimes by more exercise: cricket, perhaps, or billiards, croquet, or deck-tennis—the latter usually a foursome with nephew, wife and niece, and played in the pavilion. The time of year and weather ruled the choice.

After dinner, failing urgent necessity for more work, he would read—sometimes the most frivolous 'bloods'—for recreation, or play billiards, until the ten o'clock cup of tea and bed.

At his house in Hampstead life was naturally less regular, owing to the engagements, social and literary, on account of which he 'came up'; but the main lines were kept as far as possible. Even here he often rode or walked for a short time before breakfast, and always put in several hours of writing before lunch.

Until the last few months of his life the substantial, upright figure and bronzed face were those rather of a country squire than of a man of letters. And just a country squire he loved to be.

. . . . .

Travel had always great attraction for him. His wife's tendency to bronchial delicacy in winter made a warm climate at that time of year advisable, and all kinds of places—from Cape Town to California—were visited, in search of more

permanent health for her. Letters to myself
from many parts of the world bear witness to
their enjoyment of these trips, and to his delight
whenever their pursuit of the sun they mutually
worshipped was rewarded by improvement in her
condition.

For, in the midst of all the increasing pressure
of work and responsibility entailed by the steady
growth of his reputation, my brother's paramount
concern remained the same: care for the utmost
well-being of the beloved wife whose daily,
devoted help and comradeship were the breath
of his life for upwards of thirty years.

To her cheerfully given assistance J. G. owed it
that he was never dependent on the ministrations
of a private secretary. Publishers, translators,
agents, he has had, of course, 'galore'; but his
public and private correspondence and a vast
amount of literary spade-work have been dealt
with by the help of his wife alone. From the
outset, the first typescript, and sometimes the
second as well, from all his MSS., was typed by
her, with professional speed and skill, in daily
'doses' keeping steady pace with his production,
that he might have the benefit of a clean, fresh
script, on which to work again.

That capacity for keeping pace may be said to
have applied equally well in regard to all other
tastes and occupations.

Since the early days, when we studied under
the same professor, her considerable musical gifts
were chiefly devoted to creating for Jack the atmosphere in which he best loved to work; and all her

powers of thought and action were concentrated
on carrying out her share of the labour entailed
by the claims and functions of his profession,
with maximum efficiency, and minimum strain
to himself.

Unhappy if apart for more than a few hours at
a time, each appeared to feel the nearness of the
other indispensable to the full enjoyment of
anything.

As animal-champions, and, especially, as dog-
lovers, there has been nothing to choose between
them. As lovers of nature or art the same close
comradeship—with, naturally, occasional slight
divergences of opinion — continually obtained.
Her constant vigilance to fend off interruptions
or to prepare every small item that might facili-
tate his day's work was always as touching as his
own watchful anxiety lest she should find a room
too chilly or take cold from sitting in a draught.

.   .   .   .   .

I have often been asked: "Is—or was—Mr.
Galsworthy as wonderful as his books?"

No one, I think, who knew him at all well
would have hesitated any more than I did in
answering: "Yes—more wonderful."

But, in contradiction to the old saw: 'No
man is a hero to his valet-de-chambre', it
was most especially to the members of his
own family and household that J. G. endeared
himself.

The claims of relations, friends and strangers
alike upon his time and helpful trouble were

In the Porch with "Wolf,"
Bury House, Sussex

In the Porch with "Wolf,"
Bury House, Sussex

incessant, and he tried to fulfil them all, rarely refusing to respond in some way to any that were in the least degree reasonable. But his loyal and paternal feeling for his own family in particular was one of his strongest characteristics, and his own people know best how intensely genuine and sympathetic were all his charities, that had their root in a fatherliness of spirit which took the place of Father with us all, caring for our welfare and serving our interests with a quiet persistence so unassuming that we were never allowed to realise the long hours of drudgery it cost him.

Whatever other cares or business might be weighing on his mind, he never let one feel that he was hurried, but gave his time and attention with a beautiful leisureliness that brought a special comfort of its own.

Those who seek in my brother's writings some definite expression of religious views will be disappointed. All dogmatic theorising was alien to him. His religion was, rather, a thing to be sensed from his own personality—deduced from his whole attitude towards life and his fellowmen. The working creed that governed his own life is perhaps best summed up in the following primitive little verse by Adam Lindsay Gordon, which particularly appealed to him, and which he often quoted:

> 'Life is mostly froth and bubble;
> Two things stand like stone:
> Kindness in another's trouble,
> Courage in your own.'

And the quiet carrying out of simple yet exacting rules of conduct such as these he found to be— as he once said, diffidently—"a whole-time job."

    .   .   .   .   .

There are many reasons why his works have so wide and strong an appeal, but the most potent— as it seems to me—is this: that his characters and their developments are never superficially invented for ulterior purposes concerning plot or 'effect' of any kind, but are, in a rare degree, the spontaneous creations of his own personality, the product of his own experience, the fruit of his own observation, the flower of his own feeling.

Whether he draws a Ferrand or a Wanda, a Nedda Freeland or a Michael Mont, something deeper than imagination has gone to their making: a human spirit of rare vision and understanding has informed them and makes them touchingly alive.

People have called him a pessimist, and have said that he was one who 'failed to see a way out'.

True enough, his eyes were open to all the most tragic aspects of life. True enough, he was never known to offer a smug prescription for the cure of any ill, nor a cut-and-dried solution for any world-problem. But behind the characteristic determination to present all sides of a situation with impartial fairness, behind the consistent refusal to hand out the cheap panacea of some convenient, superficial theory, there 'grinned through' always, for such as had feelers to sense

it, the conviction that was the touchstone of his
own life: a bedrock faith in the power of *character* to solve the peculiar riddle of each individual
case.

Right for the under-dog, yes. But the judi-
cious handling of power, and the benevolent
application of wealth, in enterprise and action,
by far-seeing and well-intentioned individuals,
appealed to him as a surer means to that end
than the dissipation of all wealth into a level
sameness of impotent fractions.

Representative government — yes. But the
priceless rallying-point for human feeling offered
by a monarchy, in the safe hands of individuals
whose one thought is for the welfare of their
great family, was in his eyes a rare national
treasure which it would be the height of un-
grateful folly to depreciate.

And in his own small kingdom, to the best of
his competent ability, his convictions were carried
out; and such wealth as he possessed, whether
earned or inherited, was turned to practical
account for the benefit of all those fortunate souls
who served him or who came in any way under
his wing.

His feeling for his own country was warm and
strong, but quite devoid of narrow insular prejudice. The appreciation he felt for British characteristics in no way depended upon the fact that
it was his own countrymen who displayed them,
and he was never slow to recognise the good
points in types of other nationalities. His great
desire for rapprochement in thought and feeling

between all nations was made abundantly clear in many of his writings, as by his exertions on behalf of the P. E. N. Club, the objects of which have a definitely international basis. It is, however, probably not generally known that he earmarked the whole of his Nobel Prize of £9,000 immediately for the creation of a permanent income for that Club, to render it self-supporting, and further to promote its international activities and hospitalities.

.　　.　　.　　.　　.

From the year 1912 onwards many honours were conferred upon him.

He received the following Honorary Degrees:

LL.D.	.	St. Andrew's .	. 1922
Litt.D.	.	Manchester .	. 1927
Litt.D.	.	Dublin . .	. 1929
Litt.D.	.	Sheffield .	. 1930
Litt.D.	.	Cambridge .	. 1930
Litt.D.	.	Princeton, U.S.A. .	1931
Litt.D.	.	Oxford . .	. 1931

He received

Les Palmes d'Or, 1ière Classe, Belgium . 1919
Order of Merit 1929
Nobel Prize for Literature . . . 1932
And several lesser distinctions

He was

Member of Academic Committee of R. Soc. of Literature, and Fellow of that Body 1912
President of Founding Centre of P.E.N. Club 1921–33

President of English Association for the year	1924
Hon. Fellow of New College, Oxford	1926
Fellow of American Academy of Arts and Sciences	1926
Romanes Lecturer, Oxford	1931

In 1918 he declined a knighthood, simply considering that type of honour inappropriate to the profession of literature. The Orders and the Nobel Prize gave him and his wife great pleasure, as being direct and definite recognition of actual worth in his work. But titles as such had no attraction for them.

Snobbery in any form was, in fact, totally lacking to his make-up. He may, indeed, have carried his horror of that almost to excess. A vein of nervous shyness, a genuine modesty—often unsuspected, because belied by his self-possessed manner—made every public appearance a severe ordeal, and he was known to decline invitations from high quarters, from sheer dread of being thrust into some conspicuous position.

This sensitive shunning of publicity was one cause of his uncompromising aloofness towards the Press; another being the sturdy independence of spirit which held the value of the work itself to be the only thing that matters.

To say that he was 'above' being hurt by a malignant press criticism would be untrue; but conciliation in any form—however subtle—was, to his bedrock integrity, unthinkable, and he asked for nothing but to be left in peace.

Indeed, for the greater part of his literary life

he avoided reading his press reviews, as far as possible.

The prospect of a lecture to give would blacken his horizon for days beforehand. At one time the belief that his voice and diction failed to carry sufficiently well led to his adopting a too-carefully-mouthed style of delivery, which might have passed for a kind of affectation. This was fortunately soon discarded as unnecessary, and replaced by a more natural manner. The last lectures I heard him give could not have been surpassed for simple, unaffected directness of delivery, and the voice, so quiet in private life, fulfilled surprisingly the needs of any audience and auditorium, however large they might be.

He dreaded above all things the First Night of one of his plays. He was very seldom known to come before the curtain in response to the calls at the end of a performance, and the little speeches he made on such rare occasions were touchingly simple and unassuming—just thanks to actors and audience, nothing more. His usual habit of leaving the theatre by a back exit on the fall of the curtain must have disappointed many a 'house'; but it was the flight of sheer panic from an ordeal he could not face.

I have always grieved at his missing the heartening atmosphere of first-night receptions behind the scenes; for the love brought to bear on production of his work must, I think, be something unique in stage-life. Many a time, at such receptions, have members of his casts told me that they would rather have a small part in one of his plays than a conspicuous part elsewhere.

I think the reason for this must lie in their sense of the bed-rock sincerity essential to a successful reading even of his very smallest parts—a sincerity transforming mere play-acting into the gripping poignancy of a piece of actual life.

．　　　．　　　．　　　．　　　．

His public may, I think, be divided into four sections: those who call him sentimental, and those who do not; those who find him lacking in humour, and those who sense a subtle humour lurking in almost every page.

In order to spend a lifetime tilting at cruelties and abuses and yet escape the charge of sentimentality, he should have lived in another age. But if 'sentimentality' means—as I take it to mean —a slopping over of unrestrained and *weakly* sentiment, then the application of the term to him and his life implies merely a lack of near acquaintance with either the one or the other.

A facetious contemporary once printed a remark to the effect that Galsworthy always appeared to him to have the air of saying "How noble I am!" Perhaps only those who knew J. G. most intimately are capable of gauging the full distance by which this observation fell wide of the mark; since only such intimates might ever guess at the weight of disinclination to be combatted before he could bring himself to figure at all as the public champion of some ill-starred cause. If he could possibly help it anonymously he did so—and by return of post. His left hand never knew what his right hand had done; and in tendering his practical tokens of sympathy his great preoccupation was always to dress them in such matter-of-fact and casual guise as might be least irksome or embarrassing to the recipient.

Hundreds of persons, who, like all his family, have benefited by his unaffected encouraging kindness, will bear me out in my testimony to the level-headed, rational nature of that, and of the shrewd advice which usually accompanied it.

If his type of sympathy—his tender solicitude —was 'sentimental', then would the world be the better place were we all sentimentalists to-morrow.

To attempt to argue the point with those who have charged him with lack of humour would be futile. Humour, rightly so called—for I am not speaking of the obvious sallies of coarse wit— is an aroma of the spirit as intangible, as incapable of proof or explanation, as a flash of colour or the haunting scent of a flower.

People either feel his humour and (as often as not) the subtle pathos underlying it, or—they do not. And that, (to speak in the modern tongue) is 'all there is to it'.

.   .   .   .   .

Any detailed comment on his work would be out of place in this purposely brief and personal note, and has been left to those better equipped to undertake it.[1]

To my own lot fell, years ago, the privilege of

---

[1] I should like to record here my keen appreciation of the sympathetic and understanding study: 'John Galsworthy,' by Hermon Ould.

another task, which anyone might have fulfilled, though none, perhaps, with greater zest or love. This was the making of explanatory 'glossaries' for the use of his translators, in order to obviate the labour to himself of constantly answering letters containing lists of irksome questions.

This simple task of paraphrasing brought its own reward, entailing as it did an immediate, careful, second reading and study of every novel, play or story as it appeared, and the consequent sense of greater intimacy with many a hidden loveliness.

.   .   .   .   .

My last impression of him, at Grove Lodge, one afternoon before his illness laid him low, was a beautiful one for which I shall always be thankful.

He was thinner, and very quiet, and a curiously spiritualised look—a sort of genial radiance—was touchingly perceptible. We talked of old days and the old homes on Kingston Hill. With his usual courtesy, and more than usual sweetness, he brought me out to the door and said good-bye. I never spoke with him again.

During the weeks that followed, the rapidly increasing incapacity for speech or movement made it imperative to banish all whose presence might raise a brain-storm by rousing the wish to talk. No one might see him but his own household, doctors, and nurses.

When I saw him again he was unconscious; a few days later he was gone.

Not very many hours before he died, I stood alone in the open doorway of his room. The

D

bed had been drawn forward, so that the sunshine
he loved might fall full on the quiet form lying upon
it. By its side, equally motionless, sat the figure
of her who would not leave him till the end.

As I stood, and watched, he slowly raised his
hand.

That simple gesture was indescribably impressive
—as though some ineffably solemn vision were
passing through the barely conscious brain behind
those quiet closed eyes.

Then, the hand fell back upon the bed, and
all was still.

.   .   .   .   .

Of all his works, his poems are, perhaps, least
widely read. Yet many of them are fragrant
with the essence of his spirit.

The poem, *Valley of the Shadow*, printed on the
form used at his Memorial Service in Westminster
Abbey is one of these. But of this it should be
understood that it was written during the War, in
a passion of regretful grief on behalf of the gallant
young lives slain in the cause of world-peace.

There are two others, which, with the well-
known *Prayer*, stand to me more truly for the final
message of his own life:

ERRANTRY

Come! Let us lay a lance in rest,
And tilt at windmills under a wild sky!
For who would live so petty and unblest
That dare not tilt at something ere he die?
Rather than, screened by safe majority,
Preserve his little life to little ends,
And never raise a rebel cry!

Ah! for a weapon so sublime
That, lifted, counts no cost of woe or weal,
Since Fate demands it shivered every time!
When in the wildness of our charge we reel
Men laugh indeed—the sweeter heavens smile,
For all the world of fat prosperity
Can not outweigh that broken steel!

The echo of our challenging
Sets swinging all the bells of ribaldry,
And yet those other hidden bells that ring
The faint and wondering chimes of sympathy
Within the true cathedral of our souls.
So, crystal-clear, the shepherd's pipe will move
His browsing flock to reverie.

God save the pennon, in the morn,
That signals moon to stand, and sun to fly;
That flutters when the weak is overborne
To stem the tide of fate and certainty.
It knows not reason, and it seeks no fame,
But has engraven round its stubborn wood:
"Knight-errant, to Eternity!"

So! Undismayed beneath the clouds
Shall float the banner of forlorn defence—
A jest to the complacency of crowds,
But haloed with the one diviner sense:
To hold itself as nothing to itself;
And in the quest of the imagined star
To lose all thought of recompense.

COURAGE

Courage is but a word, and yet, of words
The only sentinel of permanence;
The ruddy watch-fire of cold winter days,

We steal its comfort, lift our weary swords,
And on. For faith—without it—has no sense;
And love to wind of doubt and tremor sways;
And life forever quaking marsh must tread.

Laws give it not; before it prayer will blush;
Hope has it not; nor pride of being true.
'Tis the mysterious soul which never yields,
But hales us on and on to breast the rush
Of all the fortunes we shall happen thro';
And when Death calls across his shadowy fields—
Dying, it answers: "Here! I am not dead!"

THE STUDY WINDOW, GROVE LODGE
1926
[*Photo by Lafayette*]

PART II

Letters from
JOHN GALSWORTHY
bearing on
Points in this Memoir

N.B.—*As these letters have no special continuity, they are placed in chronological order.*

[Five letters to Ralph Mottram]

Kingswear

May 20 1904

MY DEAR RALPH

.   .   .   .   .

We are all of us so differently made up that I hope you will never take anything I say in the light of advice, but only in the light of suggestion round which your independent spirit should play freely and reject freely. . . . You have got to find out for yourself, of course, what is your natural way of working—whether you can improve things by tinkering at them or not; as a general rule I should say things can be improved that way, and that never, or very rarely, can gems be cut perfectly at the first trial. However, this you can only find out by experiment.

.   .   .   .   .

Yours very sincerely

JOHN GALSWORTHY

16A Aubrey Walk

July 5 1904

The verse has come my way. If you were not made of the right stuff—which you are—I should hesitate to say what I think of them. It is only the common clay that cannot stand blame and (what is harder to stand) praise. I emphasise this, and please take it to heart, because if you are one of the sort (which you are not) that cannot stand praise, I will have nothing to do with you. Your verses are true poetry. I take a great responsibility in telling you that, because it means so much. So-called poetry is as common as blackberries, true poetry as rare as true chivalry —the greater portion of what is written by even 'great' poets being balderdash.

. . . Your poems have none of the essential smallness of minor poetry . . . in all those which emotionalised me most . . . is that essence of *song* which goes straight through the ear to the heart . . . and you have shown that you have the gift necessary to poetry of not too definitely picturing the thought . . .

I don't know if you do read much poetry, but if I were you I wouldn't read any more. You know quite enough about metre to set yourself to crystallising out metres of your own. [I—who know little or nothing about metre—feel instinctively that violence in them is to be avoided, and strength, sweetness, and dignity to be looked

for. You are on the natural road to these qualities . . . What is most striking of all—and
most hopeful—is that none of the poems have
been written from the head. For Heaven's sake,
under *no* circumstances, whatever happens to
you, ever write anything unless you must.

.   .   .   .   .

> Very sincerely yours
> JOHN GALSWORTHY

> 16A Aubrey Walk
> *July* 15 1904

.   .   .   .   .

There is just one thing I ought to have said to
you the other day. Have you ever considered
how much steam and motive power the hated
Bank has furnished you with—and been grateful?
To produce strong things, love and hate must be
behind. Reaction one must have.

> 16A Aubrey Walk
> *July* 19 1904

. . . With regard to writing. There are eighteen hundred novels published every year; you

may conceive what that means in MS. produced and presented for publication; but this is not in the least a depressing fact—indeed it is entirely beside the point, which is simply this: Do you or do you not find pleasure by writing? If 'no', then stop writing, if 'yes', never mind about any outside facts but go on. [The usefulness or value of what you produce will *settle itself* quite apart from you. To my mind there is no other criterion than the above. The formula is simple, apply it. Personally, I have no doubt that if you stop writing you will experience a sort of starvation. It is a thing luckily that can be combined with the leadership of cavalry, or with banking, perhaps with both . . .

Garnett's . . . general criticism or rather advice to you is: not to be afraid of cancellation, pruning and revision. "There is so much that is good plus inspiration that they ought to be cut into, strengthened, [have] everything weak or unnecessary taken out, at the expense of quantity."

.   .   .   .   .

Don't force yourself with the poems; things will come to you at happy moments . . . Don't be discouraged—and if you have a fit of reaction, don't be alarmed. We all get it.

Affectionately yours

JOHN GALSWORTHY

16A Aubrey Walk
September 20 1904

As to 'moral tendencies' we all have them, or philosophies which correspond to them—the thing we writers have to study is how to present our philosophy so that others can assimilate it without nausea—and this gilding of the pill is Art.

'Art for Art's sake'—there is no such thing— only Art for the sake of getting ourselves, our feelings, our visions known, felt and seen by a sort of ideal spectator created by our own instinct and our experience, and who is at once our conscience and our audience.

.   .   .   .   .

JOHN GALSWORTHY

[*To M. E. R.*]
[Concerning a German play that I
translated.]
[Some time during 1902 or '03]
Sunday

DEAR SWEET MAB

I wanted to say that I think my natural perverseness made me overdo my expressions about the play. It's doubtless above the average, and was worth translating—the rest is on the knees of the Gods. I have got to be very intolerant in literature, and to take for granted that we are discussing everything from the highest stand-points—this of course makes for depreciations and depressions which must be taken 'cum granis'.

Certainly I am proud of you as a translator. . . . If I may venture one remark it is that the star before you should be the beauty of words. You have now attained an extraordinary ease and natural fluency of expression—port your helm a wee bit.

I run to slang so much myself that I know where the danger lies — in striving to attain naturalness, real life semblance, one sometimes misses a certain distinction of words wherein lies their permanency.

Goodnight . . . and know that you have done good things.

Lovingly yours

JACK

[*To M. E. R.*

During the greater part of his last illness our Father lived with my husband and myself at our house, 10 Tor Gardens, Campden Hill. A few months before his death, as I was expecting my first child, Owen, he was transferred to the house of my sister, Mrs. Sauter, 1 Holland Park Avenue, where he died on December 8, 1904.]

[Some time during 1904]

Sunday

. . . Give my love to the Dad. I will be in on Tuesday about 2.45 till tea time. We don't take enough burden off your shoulders, dear soul —will try and do better, after Tuesday.

Be not discouraged in literary matters. The wind always hangs there, nor is that any *bad sign*, only a stupid and irritating condition of affairs.

Things go in streaks, so have a good courage.

Lovingly

JACK

[*To our Father*]

Turin

September 10 1904

MY DEAREST DAD

I have to-day picked up at Aosta all my lagging letters. Will you please thank the girls heartily for all their newses. I was so relieved to hear that you managed the move without harm; it was wonderfully plucky of you in the midst of such pain and weather. I am just passing through here on the way to Paris, where I arrive to-morrow. Shall be home at the end of the week—on Monday at latest . . . I spent five days at Courmayeur, but never again so wonderful a view as the first day, though I was high up every day. One must seemingly get the exact atmospheric conditions, as well as the actual mountains. The weather had gone to pieces as I came down, but nothing subdues the beauty of the Val d'Aosta, especially the lower part and towards Chatillon; there is a kind of lotus-eating look about it which I've never seen elsewhere except in the east—and that is different, too . . . The diligence driving which still survives in those valleys is full of a slow merriment of its own, which makes it infinitely preferable to train work. It's jolly to see the road before you, and fall half asleep, and wake up and munch fruit, and doze off, and wake up, and watch the vines, and throw soldi to the poor crones, and listen to a couple of Padres, droning on the back seat; all the time to the crack of the driver's whip and the jing-jing of the horses' bells.

They work their horses too young. I've seen three or four—age given at three to five years— looking like scarecrows, with bent legs and haggard eyes. The same with fruit—they pick it too young. It's rare to get a ripe peach, and a ripe pear—never. Figs are the pick of the basket; and grapes, when you have washed them . . .

It seems difficult to realise that I've seen the last of the mountains; when you have been among them a few weeks they have grown into your philosophy of things in an alarming way, haven't they?

My best love, dear, and hopes that this next week may be a better one.

Most lovingly yours
JACK

[*To Ralph Mottram*]
Dürrenstein Hotel
Platzwiese
Ampezzothal
July 6 1905

MY DEAR RALPH

Yes, isolation is better than stupefaction, which is the effect of long and painful compromise. I'm exceedingly thankful I was of much slower growth than you, and hadn't sloughed off my skin at college and after. The sloughing process is most painful . . . The world is made up— *me judice*—to each of us, of about, say, three people who can and will and do understand and go with one, a number of people with whom one can fraternise on one point or two; and the rest— who are merely specimens under glass cases to be scrutinised, impartially if possible, as we pass by. I don't in the least mean to preach pride and prejudice and want of sympathy; I only mean to say that we must take ourselves and others as we are, and not fret because we are not alike.

.   .   .   .   .

[The one precious thing in life (except love) is the impersonal eye, the eye that looks on things from the outside; and to keep this eye bright is far more important and entrancing than any amount of companionship. Our philosophy should be to combine this eye with mental indulgence towards all those phenomena one is looking at, and with practical sympathy for all kinds of real suffering.

.   .   .   .   .

I am always being pulled-up by the difficulty of reconciling two opposite laws which seem to govern every problem and thing one looks at. For instance, the longer one lives the more one sees that everything is form, taste, the way a thing is done—and yet at the same time the more one recognises that the only thing that matters is the spirit that moves the man.

Anyway, I can't make my meaning clear, for the weather is terrible hot.

.   .   .   .   .

Affectionately yours

J. G.

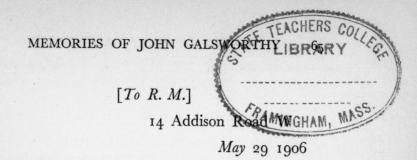

[*To R. M.*]

14 Addison Road W

May 29 1906

Got yours this morning, and have been through it all. It's really splendid stuff seen together like this—it's a real delight to me to read your verse.

As to your collapse, my dear boy, the discovery you have made is the most cheering thing in the world. If it were not as you say, there would be no such thing as Art, and we should all be floating around skyscraping in clouds of our own wool.

You want a little Mozart, Gluck, and Anatole France to steady you, and make you fall in love again with the golden fields of the tiny, trivial, superficial, physical *detail*—which, by the way, is none of these epithets, and which is all the salt.

.   .   .   .   .

Yours

J. G.

E

[*To M. E. R.*

On the advent of my second child, Veronica.]

8 South Terrace

Littlehampton

July 30 1907

DEAR SWEET MAB

Warmest love, and thanks for such a charming thing . . . How delicious to be over it, for both of you! It is so nice to think of it as past, and peace about your heads. Bless you! My warm felicitations to Tom. We had meant to be in London for the event. We shall be up on Saturday and come to you on Sunday to see if we may have a look.

May the little 'un have all your courage; and a life of sun.

Ever most lovingly, dear Sweet,

Your

JACK

M. E. R. AND VERONICA
1910

[To Mr. Arthur Ponsonby, now Lord Ponsonby of Shulbrede]

14 Addison Road W

September 18 1907

MY DEAR PONSONBY

.   .   .   .   .

Candidly and between ourselves, I wish to avoid all label of party, which I think sits ill on the back of one who tries to be an artist and present impartially what seems to him the truth in life and character. I try to be and to keep in the middle of things, and to strike at what seems to me redundant and extravagant on either side. This is what I humbly think is the function of art in its negative and satiric form.

.   .   .   .   .

JOHN GALSWORTHY

[To R. M.]

Wingstone

May 8 1908

MY DEAR RALPH

.   .   .   .   .

The reason . . . is that you do not believe in trying to put back the clock. Regret nothing, and go forward; *voilà tout!* Life's nothing but change of form to form, in which each age plays its own peculiar part, and all that matters, as it seems to me, is to make that part a strenuous one. As to free will and determinism—it's an obvious case of 'a little bit of both' . . .

The persons who leave the beaten track are generally beaten themselves by lack of moral courage. The persons like your Dad and old Jolyon (the best types of those who remain in) have lots of moral courage, but not much spiritual. That is to say, their objective is constitutionally one which does not take them out of the beaten track. They have all the drag of the high road, and lots of moral grit to take them through it. But the finest type of all of course (and very very rare) is he who constitutionally takes the path of exploration, and has also the moral grit to carry his exploration through, living a fine life.

.   .   .   .   .

Yours

J. G.

[*To Mrs. Scott, who became Lady Hilton-Young and later Lady Kennet*]

Wingstone

December 7 1909

DEAR MRS. SCOTT

I am waiting for . . . the decision in 'closed-cell' confinement.

What you say cheers me, but I shall not believe till I hear with my own ears, and see with my own eyes that this horror has been done away with. No one who hasn't seen and through seeing felt with those poor creatures, can tell what incalculable misery it will remove—if it really comes to pass. Herbert Gladstone will deserve honour in the land, if he does really bring it about. It makes me sick to think of the money, time and talk, wasted on things that are six of one and half a dozen of the other, when there's real solid unnecessary misery inflicted wholesale, year in and year out, for want of a little imagination.

.   .   .   .   .

Most sincerely yours

J. G.

[As I think is well known, his labours with regard to this matter, coupled with the effect of his play *Justice*, resulted, during the winter months of 1909–10, in a great reduction of the various terms of solitary confinement.]

[*To the American publisher, Mr. Alfred Knopf*]

14 Addison Road   W.

February 15 1911

DEAR MR. KNOPF

Thank you very warmly for your letter . . . Of course there are differences of judgment between us, but I think you are right in placing *The Man of Property* and *Fraternity* at the top of the novels. I don't know whether I agree that *Justice* is superior to *Strife*; it is in spirit, I think, but is not the equal of *Strife* in its dramatic quality.

.   .   .   .   .

Yours very truly

JOHN GALSWORTHY

[*To M. E. R.*

Concerning the Manchester production of 'The Little Dream']

Midland Hotel

Manchester

April 5 1911

DEAREST MAB

. . . The little play is promising better than I hoped. The Seelchen is perfect—dances good —music could not be better.

Seen to-day, dimly lighted, the mountain group was beautiful—remains to be seen how it will look when the light brightens; but anyway the faces are quite fine, though we've had a struggle with them. They are all working with a will and little von B. is as pleased as Punch. I owe you a great debt for getting me this music[1]; the

---

[1] By Wolfgang von Bartels.

LILIAN WITH HER SON, RUDOLF

J. G. WITH OWEN, VERONICA AND "CHRIS"
("The Spaniel John")

greatest stroke of theatrical luck I am ever likely to have.

I may see you on Sunday . . .

Your loving

JACK

Iden Payne—the director—is delighted with the music.

[*To A. K.*]

Wingstone

May 16 1911

DEAR MR. KNOPF

. . . . .

In pondering the vexed question: what is drama, what is the ideal play, I am often—personally—inclined to throw over all canons and merely to ask myself whether there is any test but that of effect. All the rest at times seems pure petty, momentary academics. To stir human nature is the prime test, I think, for to really stir human nature a work of art must ring absolutely true, must have lost all the feeling of fake and manufacture so highly prized by the academic. One thing at all events we know very well—that the ideal *manufacture* of to-day's plays will be the

vieux jeu of to-morrow's. Cf. Ibsen. For Ibsen
is *vieux jeu, except* for the stir he sets up in one.

.   .   .   .   .

Yours very truly
JOHN GALSWORTHY

[*To A. K.*]
Wingstone
June 14 1911

I thought my letter conveyed the impression (or
rather I meant it to) that to the purely academic
follower of technique Ibsen's technique was already
old-fashioned. It is Ibsen's spirit, and the truth
of what he said which makes Ibsen great, not the
precise form in which he said it. There is every
hope for any dramatist who has depth and sincerity of feeling and clearness of vision, and has also
a power of expression (whatever its form) to con-
vey to his audience the impression of these qualities. There is no hope for any other sort of
dramatist, however skilful he may be—however
'well-made' his plays. It is the temperament,
the philosophy, of the dramatist that matters—
and to exhibit his *spirit* he may choose what subjects and take what forms he likes.

If he does not see deep enough and with a sort

of 'world vision' he cannot possibly last.   Ibsen did—so he will last.

With very kind regards I am

Yours sincerely

JOHN GALSWORTHY

[*To A. K.*]

Wingstone

July 2 1912

It was very jolly of you to send us that photo. We hate it like anything, but it makes our guests laugh, and the weather is so wet.   It gives me white eyebrows, no hair at all except a beautiful clump where I ought to have had it cut by the sheep shearers, and an expression more mad than even by right belongs to me.   To her, it gives the aspect of one saying 'Look here!   You will not blarney me with that smile—I am off to do some civic work!'

We shall shoot at it this afternoon with an air gun.   As for you, you will frame and hang it above your copy of *The Four Winds*, and when any admirer of mine comes along you will point to them and say: Ah! but that's what he really is!

.   .   .   .   .

Sincerely yours

JOHN GALSWORTHY

[*To M. E. R.*

Concerning the scenery for the later
London production of 'The Little Dream']

Cortina

August 2 1912

DEAREST MAB

How are you all? We both flourish here. I went up the Nuvolau yesterday—a twenty mile day; and have had other good walks. Also I work.

The sketch Bruckman so kindly made for Scene 2 is a very charming picture, but unfortunately it reverts to what I wish to abandon for that scene. It is the Manchester setting, *without* faces, only better, of course. I have given that up. I want nothing but blue blackness, and, high up, just three white peaks (without faces) lighted with different colours when they speak, from behind; with the actors standing invisible in the blue blackness in front of them. I mean to . . . try this as the *simplest* possible thing; and probably the most mysterious and *least* realistic. The whole thing is to be as simple as possible.

. . . . . .

J.

[*To M. E. R.*]

Riffel Alp

August 12 1913

I promised you the enclosed—only for yourself or Tom to read, since the book won't be out till Oct. 23 . . .

We remain faithful to the Tyrol, in spite of the much greater expanse of snow here, in spite, even, of that really great mountain the Matterhorn, which looks wonderful nearly always, and has the animistic quality we have learned to look for in Nature. But the whole country has little or none of the essential charm and pagan flavour of the Southern Tyrol.

We were up at the Gornergrat yesterday with the Bird [Lilian]. It's a marvellous panorama, but though at dawn it must be really beautiful, it's too much 'twopence coloured' at 4 o'clock of a fineish afternoon—the mountains are not mysterious enough. Also fifty people on a circular platform, a railway, a dungeon of an hotel, and a stream of people going up and down recalls Hampstead of a Sunday. But for the people, mostly English, we are very well off at the Riffel Alp, but go on to Montana on Saturday at latest.

· · · · · ·

J.

[*To our cousin Dorothy Easton, later Mrs. Ivens*]

Wingstone

Manaton

Devon

September 15 1912

DEAREST DOROTHY

Stick to it and don't be discouraged—all creative work comes in gusts, and fits, and starts, and puffs.

.   .   .   .   .

Our love to you

J. G.

[*To A. K.*]

14 Addison Road   W.

October 29 1912

DEAR MR. KNOPF

.   .   .   .   .

I say—I say—what are you about—writing such nice notices of my books! This will never do—even though they warm the heart of this scribe.

May the firm of Doubleday and Page never have a shadow—or if it has, may it never grow less while you are in it.

.   .   .   .   .

JOHN GALSWORTHY

[*To D. E.*]
Wingstone
November 2 1912

DEAREST DOROTHY

I'm glad you are dissatisfied—it is very healthy to be dissatisfied. I try to be all the time, and generally succeed, I can assure you.

.   .   .   .   .

J. G.

[*To D. E.*]
July 10 1913

I'm in the same sort of backwater myself. These phases pass.

.   .   .   .   .

J. G.

[*To Professor Gilbert Murray*]
Wingstone
November 3 1912

MY DEAR MURRAY

.   .   .   .   .

I had a beastly time in London and elsewhere for nearly three weeks—lecturing in the North, production of *The Pigeon* at Liverpool—quite good—*Eldest Son* in London, dentist, and visits to slaughter-houses—very gruesome. I have written two articles. May I send them to you to run a critical eye over? And where shall I try to plant them—*The Times*? I'm in touch with Dr. Addison, who will stir the House up when they appear.

.   .   .   .   .

J. G.

[*To an unrecorded correspondent*]

14 Addison Road   W.

July 16 190?

MY DEAR MADAM

.   .   .   .   .

You ask for some glimpse of a road leading away definitely from the morass of un-fraternity which my book discloses as quaking under our feet. There is no definite road. There's only a feeling in the heart. Everyone knows what that feeling is or ought to be—it's the common-place of Christianity, which religion, if dead (and I think rightly dead), in its dogmas, is living enough (perhaps never more so) in its essence.

The more *definitely* constructive a *novelist* becomes in all matters of social import, the less convincing he is bound to be. What does the poet say:

"There are fifty-seven ways
  Of writing tribal lays,
  And every blessed one of them is right!"?

or wrong. The only thing that matters, and the only thing that remains, is the spirit underlying them. My method is to suggest that the spirit of understanding and sympathy ought to be there by pointing out that it is not. I think that by this method one gets less on the nerves of one's reader. Moreover, it's temperamental—to preach directly I am not able—however confirmed a moralist I may be by deduction.

. . . There have been spasms of fraternity in the world more acute than we have with us now, and dating from before the time of Christ; but I think that there has probably been no time in which the notion of fraternity has been more general and diffused than now, in spite of all the signs to the contrary.

If you read *The Man of Property* or *The Island Pharisees* or even *The Country House*, you will see that I always pursue the negative method; and though I'm continually charged with not showing the way to Heaven, I believe that I do set up a process in people's spirits, which makes them rather more alive to the Pharisaism, sense of property, intolerance, and humbug, which stand in the way of sympathy between man and man.

Please accept my hearty thanks for your letter, and believe me,

Sincerely yours
JOHN GALSWORTHY

[*To an unrecorded correspondent*]

Wingstone

December 11 1912

DEAR MADAM

.   .   .   .   .

There are for me no water-tight compartments in human life . . . Any glib assumption of superiority is detestable, and I suppose I am always consciously or unconsciously up against it.

.   .   .   .   .

My purpose in writing? I haven't any conscious purpose except to express myself, my feelings, my temperament, my vision of what life is. I don't address any particular audience—and I don't care what lessons or morals people get out of my writings. Those who have sufficient similarity to myself in their composition will be moved to a sort of general sympathy—those who have not will reject me.

.   .   .   .   .

There is no such thing to my mind as beauty of life and conduct based on hope of reward. Beauty only lies in worship of Perfection for Perfection's sake. Perhaps *The Inn of Tranquillity* will help you to get at the core of my too unsatisfactory self.

Yours very truly

JOHN GALSWORTHY

[*To an unrecorded correspondent*]

Wingstone

November 5

MY DEAR SIR

.   .   .   .   .

As to *A Christian*: You see, to anyone who rejects as untenable the actual divinity of Christ, it is, I think, impossible to do more than accept and reverence a certain proportion of his sayings. Where, as they freely do, they contradict each other, in spirit if not in actual word, one has to sieve out for oneself an essence that best accords with one's own nature.

I have so often found that the upholders of the unhappy marriage have no leg to stand on the moment they get away from a fundamental belief in the value of martyrdom—a belief that I regard with the detestation that I have for all forms of fanaticism. In this age I think we all have to find ourselves—no glib formulas will help us, and those people who believe in flogging the dead horses of outworn religions are dead wood in our tree.

.   .   .   .   .

Yours very truly

JOHN GALSWORTHY

F

[*To J. W. Hills*]
Hotel du Moulleau
près Arcachon
France
January 11 1913

MY DEAR JACK

I am always so glad to see your fist and still more to see your face. Do you know it's almost a year since we saw each other.

.   .   .   .   .

The fact is, Life slips by, and the few people one cares to see one never sees; and that's bad.— I'm awfully glad to have your book. I badly wanted something that would tell me where we'd got to with Poor Law Reform; and now I hope I've got it. It always cheers and slightly inebriates me to feel that you are going for the real things in politics . . . It's good of you to say you'll lend a hand with the Slaughtering reform. I've just corrected proofs of the articles in pamphlet form . . . I want a very short simple Bill embodying, roughly speaking, the proposals in the articles, with possible extension of Local Authorities' powers to build Public abattoirs and close private slaughter houses in places where there are public ones.

.   .   .   .   .

All fortune to you, my very dear fellow, this year and for many to come.

Always yours affectionately
JOHN GALSWORTHY

J. G. on "Peggy" at Wingstone
1918

[*To D. E.*]

Wingstone
November 1 1913

MY DEAR DOROTHY

Very wild weather here, but wonderful light suffusing the clouds and all the colours of the hills.

Justice was very warmly received in Vienna, and so was I. We went on to Wiesbaden, I hoping to cure a rather 'sprung' arm, but without success. As generally after finishing a novel I'm finding it awfully hard to settle to another—keep writing little things—anything to get away from stiff, coherent creative thought. Bad!

Good luck to your work and wanderings.

.   .   .   .   .

J. G.

[*To D. E.*]

Wingstone
November 7 1913

You'll see by the typed copy with this how I think the play ought to run up to the point where I've made the long pencil note on your MS. as to the construction of the rest.

It's very alive—when all the self-consciousness has been taken out of it like this—and if you can screw yourself up to deal with the end of the lines I suggest, it ought to play well. . . . The thing is to get the truth and depth of it.

　　·　　　·　　　·　　　·　　　·

By careful study of the revised text with the old you will learn a lot about what is legitimate and what is superfluous on the stage. On the stage very little *well placed* does an enormous amount of work. It is largely the art of suggestion, of making the audience themselves do the work for you.

Our love to you, and good luck, my dear.

J. G.

[*To M. E. R.*]

Wingstone

Manaton

Devon

November 8 1913

DEAREST MAB

　　·　　　·　　　·　　　·　　　·

I should think nothing will be done in regard to the Library Censorship—authors are like porcupines. But I don't know.

Professional criticism is queer stuff—it's really a very unsound feature of modern life. A great

pity the writer can't find his public without it.
One learns to be a little fatalistic in regard to
one's value (if any).   What will last—will.

·   ·   ·   ·   ·

J.

[*To M. E. R.*
Referring to a letter from myself asking if
nothing could be done to make the caging of
larks or any wild song birds illegal?]
Flat 1A
Adelphi Terrace House
March 8 1914

About wild song birds . . . The Plumage
Bill does *not* include a clause dealing with larks
etc. Ada will write to (W. H.) Hudson and ask
which member he recommends.
I myself will no doubt be persona very ingrata
to M.P.'s for some time to come. Not that I
was attacking them, only what they allow Parlia-
ment to make of their instincts and energies.

·   ·   ·   ·   ·

. . . JACK
[This also refers to his letter to *The Times* of
a previous date exposing the slackness of Parlia-
ment in regard to the reform of ten crying abuses.]

[*To A. K.*]

Wingstone

June 9 1914

MY DEAR KNOPF

Very glad to have your letter, and the news of Hudson's book. It's queer to me if there isn't a large inner public for his work.

. . . . .

The artist theory of life is, of course, the right one; but to my mind it's wrong to confine it merely to work. It wants to be applied to everything—play, sleep, love, and eating. In other words, so to live that you do everything with all your heart, and have no time or inclination left for megrims or nerves. 'No excess' is inherent in this theory of life, for excess either dulls the appetite or gives you fever. So to live that you are practically unconscious that you've got to die. This is a translation into practice of the formula 'be true to your best self' if one takes a wide and sane view of what is one's best self.

The performance of this theory of life, to be effective, has got to become practically instinctive, even if it didn't start so. You have to be in training without knowing you are; so as to get rid of introspection, morbidity, and speculations on what to do with life.

Enough! Good luck to you.

Yours sincerely

JOHN GALSWORTHY

[*To D. E.*]

Wingstone .

August 8 1914

MY DEAR DOROTHY

All we peace-lovers are adrift—I as much as anyone.   Only 'general brotherliness' is any good as a thought.

.   .   .   .   .   .

Some work will turn up for you anyway.   Don't worry too much.

One is doubtful how much one will have to spare from all the appeals there will be, but if you all get very hard pushed, let me know.

Our love to you

J. G.

[*To M. E. R.*

Concerning 'War-work' and 'Unemployment', early in the War.]

Wingstone

Manaton

Devon

August 25 1914

DEAREST MAB

Yes.   Quite true.   Nothing will stop some of these well-off women from doing the work them-selves instead of paying others; because they say

it's the only way they can feel they've done something personally to help.   It's a feeling one under-
stands, but it's clearly wrong.   Ada, who first
began making nightshirts, has given it up, and is
sending stuff and payment to out-of-works.   I feel
that the whole thing has got to shake itself down
for another two months at least, before relief can
do very much in the right quarters.   It's rather a
case of dislocation of employment, than of unemployment, I expect.

The whole thing is too ghastly.

.   .   .   .   .

J.

[*To M. E. R.*]

Wingstone

September 25 1914

. . . We shan't be coming up till I've finished
my novel—soon now, I hope.   I've secured from
America £1,500 for the serial rights of it, which
will be useful for Relief Funds.   I thought it was
the best thing I could do for the moment; apart
from that inducement I couldn't have driven on
with it in this stress.

It is difficult to keep the ideal of truth bright
before one's eyes, when one's feelings are being
so harrowed by tales of atrocity.   Though much
I'm afraid is true, there are indications that

much is false; and one must struggle not to be stampeded, always remembering that the Press of every country is a miracle of unscrupulous partizanship (with a few—very few—bright exceptions, perhaps). . . .

JACK

[*To M. E. R.*]

Wingstone

October 19 1914

I send you a measly five pounds [for the Belgian refugees who came daily to our house].

The fact is, for the moment I'm depleted—having shelled out £1,000 to War Funds of sorts, besides certain private help. In two or three weeks I hope to get half my serial paid and then I'll send you something substantial.

.   .   .   .   .

J.

[*To M. E. R.*]

Wingstone

November 6 1914

Here's the cheque. Bless you.

Your loving

J.

[*To D. E.*]
Craiglands
Ilkley
Yorkshire
December 3 1914

MY DEAR DOROTHY

Yes—friendships with the simple are of the flowers of life.

.   .   .   .   .

J. G.

[*To M. E. R.*

Referring to a letter I had written to *The Times* protesting against the then prevalent injustice of visiting the national animus of war-time on perfectly blameless foreign artists (notably musicians)—a course which has always appeared to me as illogical as the indiscriminate worship of foreign artists *as such* which prevails in this country in peace-time.]

Wingstone
October 9 1914

DEAREST MAB

We read your letter in *The Times* with sympathy and interest. It is ill carrying war feelings into the region of the arts.

.   .   .   .   .

Democracy: Yes—a king (such as ours) is a boon to a democracy. It would take much ink and paper to explain what I feel on the whole of that matter, and I'd rather do it with my tongue some time.

·　　·　　·　　·　　·

Your

J.

[*To M. E. R.*

A friend had written begging me to get him to join the Committee of a certain Society. I forwarded the letter, adding a remark to the effect that I felt sure he would prefer not to do so.]

Wingstone

January 27 1915

I'm very sorry, but it *is* so—I do feel more useful keeping free of Societies.

Honestly I'm afraid all these leagues are but the outcome of the feeling so many people have that they must be doing something to help, and have no more relation to the facts of the European Situation than the Hague Conferences had before the war began.

As I said in that letter to Chevrillon (in the *Chronicle*) my only hope is in the spread of democracy, in the sense that we, France, Switzerland, Scandinavia, etc., understand the word.

·　　·　　·　　·　　·

Your

J.

[*To M. E. R.*]
                                        Wingstone
                                    June 3 1915

Warmest thanks for your sweet letter. Yes,
'Frances Freeland' is more living than 'A Portrait' [his study of our father in *A Motley*]—that
was a little too cataloguey. 'Old Jolyon' is the
real pendant to her [our mother].

.   .   .   .   .

                                        Yours
                                            J.

[*To Professor Gilbert Murray*]
                                        Wingstone
                                    July 16 1915
MY DEAR G. M.
        .   .   .   .   .

I'm reading some of the younger Russians—
Kuprin and Artibasheff. The latter's *Sanine* is
conceived in a mood that I sometimes feel this
war will leave us all: 'What's the good of anyfink?
—why nofink!' Perhaps Art will survive, and
that's all; but that means a goodish bit.

        .   .   .   .   .

                                    Always yours
                                            J. G.

[*To an unnamed correspondent*]
Wingstone

May 27 1916

MY DEAR SIR

.   .   .   .   .

It is the dogmatic and superstitional part of Christianity that the war will destroy—it was already nearly dead—not the ethical, (which is also the spiritual in the broad sense of both words). On the contrary, it will give to that, I think, a vigorous push.

.   .   .   .   .

Yours very truly

JOHN GALSWORTHY

[*To M. E. R.*]
Wingstone

July 6 1916

DEAREST MAB

. . . Did I tell you that I'm issuing a volume of 'wild oats'—humanist writings—as you wanted —in September. It's called *A Sheaf of Wild Oats.* I thought after all I might as well make what money I could out of them for funds.

.   .   .   .   .

Your

J.

[*To M. E. R.*]
1A Adelphi Terrace House
September 13 1916

Yes, we shall be here till September 25th, and very glad to see you. Ring up when you get home.

.   .   .   .   .

I offered 8 Cambridge Gate [our old house] to be a club for work and recreation for soldiers in hospital, with a personal offer to fit it up myself. They may accept . . . I went over the old house on Sunday. It's a whacker when it's empty.

.   .   .   .   .

Your
J.

[*To M. E. R.*]
Hôpital Benevole
Martouret
Die
Drôme
France
November 26*th* 1916

. . . We've had a jolly good week, and are very fit. To-day—the day of rest—we went with four of our patients up a little mountain.

My massage seems—oddly enough—to be of some use. I do about ten patients a day, about five hours in all, and half an hour's Muller exercises with some of the men, and help serve the dinner.

Ada does linen and sews pretty well all day long except from one till four-thirty.

The people are awfully nice, and the men charming; and the natives pleasant, and the country queer and beautiful.

About 8 Cambridge Gate. I certainly *wouldn't* like it called Galsworthy House; and I really don't see how I can let it be described as lent by me when it's lent by all of us. I'll pay the rates, and shall be able to send a hundred or two towards the fitting up.

.   .   .   .   .

Your

J.

[*To Monsieur André Chevrillon*]
Hôpital Benevole
Martouret
December 3 1916

MY DEAR CHEVRILLON

.   .   .   .   .

Yes, I shall get a little at the thoughts of your soldiers in time—they are not inexpressive like our Tommies—on the contrary, they talk so much that they almost paralyse my massage. The

effort to understand is considerable—given a
certain patois to overcome.

I was very interested in your 'Germany and the
War', full of depth and knowledge. The only
criticism I would make is the very general one
that I think one is a little too prone to consider
that literature has more influence than it really
has on national thought and action. The two
things go alongside each other rather than as
cause and effect, and both are the children of
material events. One remembers *The National
Review* before the war, in England, and in what an
absolute backwater it was—so, in a sense, were
the German jingos. The difference between the
two countries, I think, was rather in the fact that
in England the national head was not swelling,
and in Germany it was, and bloodheat rising.

. . . . .

Always yours

J. GALSWORTHY

[*To Professor Gilbert Murray*]

Wingstone

May 19 1917

MY DEAR G. M.

I finished the Asylum stories last night, and
got your letter this morning. I read them with
a sort of horrified interest, and, allowing for
personal animus and exaggeration, I should think

there is a horrible lot of truth in them. Institutions are almost always the devil—fearful corruptors of human nature.

I don't know what to advise. My impression is that they should be re-written, leaving out abuse, and cutting down to a minimum the exhortations. They would be much more telling as simple narrations of fact, and besides, I don't think any publisher would take them as they stand. . . . On the general question, it looks to me—without having had a chance yet to go into the law and facts of lunacy—as if what was wanted were a new Law, making monthly or bi-monthly inspection of all asylums, private and public, necessary, by a doctor and a layman, carefully selected and governmentally appointed, having no connection whatever with, and no responsibility to the Lunacy authorities, and whose duties would be to interview privately every patient in or out of the presence of their relatives, according as the relatives turned up for the inspection or not. I do think it's a most damnable thing that people's liberty should ever be in the hands of those who may be interested in keeping them in limbo. There is one point not touched on by these sketches that has always enraged me, and that is the certification for lunacy of *paupers* by a single doctor, instead of the two required for the more fortunate beings.

.   .   .   .   .

Yours always

J. G.

G

[To M. E. R.

Referring to a discussion concerning various aspects of love in literature]

Midland Hotel

Manchester

October 5 1917

MY DEAREST MAB

.   .   .   .   .

The whole question is one of infinite variety, with many turns and twists of temperamental and philosophical feeling in this writer. Of course I always have used the negative method—(I suspect because I *can't* use the other)—deliberately, from the hatred of preaching; from a sort of natural disgust at setting up to being a teacher on a lofty moral plane. . . . Excess I can and do condemn, and a yielding to passion where it causes great pain to others; but I feel it all to be a question of balance. . . . I recognise passion as *the* great natural instinct . . . a glow in human life, a good and not an evil. . . . On the other hand, I do feel that 'earthly' love between two people carries in itself as fearful possibilities of destruction as does the suppression of that natural instinct. In other words, it's always 'excess' at which, as a thinker and a writer, I aim my shafts.

.   .   .   .   .

J.

[*To* M. E. R.
Concerning the declined Knighthood]
Beach Hotel
Littlehampton
January 3 1918

This has been a queer little typhoon in a tea-
cup. You may well have rubbed your eyes . . .
but all over now, except a general sense of being
thought a churl or a prig by those who don't
understand.

'Letters' are so utterly apart from titles and
such . . .; but how many realise that?

    .   .   .   .   .

J.

I only got a wire about the Knighthood at
9.30 p.m. on New Year's Eve, and wired off
refusal at once—too late.

[*To* D. E.]
Wingstone
May 30 1918

MY DEAR DOROTHY

I admire the way you stick to it, and mean to
do only the very best that is in you. That's the
way. Oh yes! black times, but they pass; and
one good book is worth a dozen cheap and easy

ones, and makes a writer's name, whereas the cheap ones don't.

.   .   .   .   .

Yours always

J. G.

[*To M. E. R.*]

Villa Margherita
Charleston

March 19 1919

My Dear Mab

. . . Until this last week we have not had time to turn round here. I spoke eighteen times in about as many days, taking in New York, Boston, Philadelphia, Princeton and Washington. Down here it's very quaint, lovely and restful, and we go on to-morrow to a South Carolina Plantation, thence to Asheville, capital of North Carolina, before beginning my lecturing tour again at Cincinnati on April 2nd. I'm giving what I make by lecturing, above our expenses, to Syrian and Armenian etc. relief . . . Having a very jolly time here in the South. Ada well.

.   .   .   .   .

J. G.

[*To M. E. R.*]
> The Manor
>> Albemarle Park
>>> Asheville   N.C.

April 1 1919

. . . . .

We have had an excellent holiday in the Carolinas. Here it's fine mountain country, with a wonderful blue in the quality of the scenery.

To-day we go on to Cincinnati and many other towns to lecture, and reach New York again on April 19th, where I shall have to speak another seven times before we take steamer home.

We do hope you are all going on serenely. I am wondering very much about Lily and the boy, and all that is happening—perhaps nothing.

. . . . .

J. G.

[*To his nephew, Hubert John Galsworthy*]
> Wingstone

October 14 1919

DEAREST HUBERT

Yes, I got your letter written at the beginning of term, and my conscience has often been bad since, but it's always recovered too soon. We're

back here now, alone, but for the five dogs and
one cat all putting their paws in my eye while
I write. Trywell, the hound puppy, is 'looking
up' (as they say) 'fine'! What would you do if
you had just received a letter from a strange lady
in Louisiana (United States of America, *vide* your
superior knowledge) with red hair and five children, who says she wants to be your friend, because
something about your mouth makes her think you
don't like sleep? This comes of being infamous
and having one's photo published in magazines.

Pause here, to give Trywell three small biscuits
and one large smack with a copy of *The New World*.
I hope the weather at Xmas will be as nice for
you here as it is now. You will find the robins
come in friendly if you encourage them. I used
to have one perching on my writing table and
almost feeding out of my hand the two winters
we spent here. Your Aunt joins me in best love.
My nib is giving up the ghost.

Your always affectionate Uncle

JACK

Let's hear how you go on getting out of that
form, which is always a most excellent thing to
do. How do you like letters to be addressed to
you? Esq., or Mister, or simply plain, like this
one?

[*To* H. J. G.]

Hotel Reina Cristina
Algeciras
Spain
Feb. 3 1920

DEAREST HUBERT

So very glad you all had a good time at Wingstone, and that you were able to write a lot.

We are enjoying Spain very much. Your Auntie is quite well again. We spent one night at San Sebastian (raining); and one in Madrid to see the pictures in the Prado (Velasquez and Goya are the two great Spanish painters, and there are many of their pictures there); then we were four days in Seville, a wonderfully picturesque old town, with a glorious Cathedral, which took one hundred and fifty years to build (1400–1550) and has the finest interior of any Church, I think, in the world. In Seville we saw a street which has the name Orfila.

From Seville we went to Malaga (12 hours train to do 120 miles). It's a lively town and port, and the hotel was in a street, and all exuberant gentlemen came and shouted at the tops of their voices in a sort of bar across the way from 10 p.m. to 2 a.m., when a sudden silence would fall. It was jolly walking on the hillsides and valleysides about there covered with fruit trees *in blossom*, olives, and goats. This is a great country for goats and donkeys. The dogs are a poor lot.

But I think animals and children are well treated on the whole everywhere.

We stayed a fortnight at Malaga and then came on here opposite Gibraltar, which lies out like a great lion. It makes one feel what awful cheek the English have. It's just as if the Spanish owned the Isle of Wight, or St. Michael's Mount off Penzance. It's a lovely hotel in a lovely garden—this, and the country round is green and very like South Ireland, with little white-washed houses very like Irish cabins surrounded by pigs (red-brown pigs) and poultry. And the people aren't very unlike the Southern Irish either; after all, they were both of the Iberian race originally. The queer thing is that Algeciras means 'the emerald isle', which is of course the pet name we give to Ireland. From here we go to Ronda; Granada; Cordoba; Valencia; Barcelona (see map). It's a beautiful interesting country altogether.

We expect to be back at Grove Lodge about the middle of March. You will all be going to Wingstone again for the Easter holidays no doubt.

Ever your very affectionate Uncle

J. G.

[*To M. E. R.*

A typical response]

Grove Lodge
Hampstead
October 10 1920

DEAREST MAB

Here is the £50. . . . If Mrs. — repays
you, you can repay me. You needn't mention
me in the matter.

Your loving

J.

[*To M. E. R.*]

Hotel Chatham
New York
November 13 1920

Just a line from this comparatively near spot
before we start across. We go on Monday by
way of Chicago, Denver, Salt Lake City and Los
Angeles to Santa Barbara.

We have been in the country the last six days
at various very pretty places staying with friends.
The weather is most lovely.

The Skin Game is a great success, they say—
though the performance is not up to that in
London. *The Mob*, on the other hand, running

at the Neighbourhood Playhouse is a fine production, and the run has been lengthened from an
original 4 weeks to 8 weeks owing to the demand.
The theatre is a small repertory theatre, so that
this is quite phenomenal.

Everybody is awfully kind as usual; and this
hotel very homey. All the personnel the same
as last year, and glad to see one. Ada is tired,
but fairly well. We shall be at Santa Barbara
10 weeks, and I hope she will get rested there
. . . Any news always received with joy.

. . .

J.

[*To* M. E. R.]

San Ysidro Ranch
Santa Barbara
California
December 3 1920

We were so sorry to hear of the head troubling
you again.   Don't you think you ought to osteopath again? Two years' relief was something,
anyway.   If any question of economy is blocking
the way, my child, please let me make you a little
Xmas present of the treatment.   Do!   Write and
let me know you've started in.   It would be
hateful to think that you were suffering avoid-
ably.

It's distressing that Tom is having such bad
luck.   He suffers from his loyalty to sinking

ships . . . So glad the children are well. Give
them our love at Xmas and the enclosed small
gift divided up.

We continue to have lovely weather here. I
write pretty steadily, and in the afternoon we walk,
or I play tennis. The evenings one reads and
writes letters—a very quiet existence. The people
all quite nice and friendly. So glad you liked
In Chancery . . . I'm not lecturing this time—
except that I to-day agreed to go and give an
address to the University Fine Arts Society at
San Francisco on December 27.

. . . bless you . . .

Your most loving

J. G.

Do go and osteopath!

[*To M. E. R.*]

Santa Barbara

January 21 1921

.   .   .   .   .

Santa Barbara, or rather, Montecito, which is
our country end of it, is certainly very beautiful.
The mountains . . . green, *not* snow mountains,
lie back from the Pacific beach about three miles,
and all the ground in between is a gradually

rising tangle of orange, lemon, eucalyptus, live-oak, palm, plane, pepper and pine-trees, mimosas, guavas and grape-fruits.   The climate is certainly good and very sunny.

I've finished a 3 act comedy, a one act comedy, and two short stories here; and feel rather emptied out.   Ada is beginning, I think, to have more steam in her.   *The Skin Game* and *The Mob* still go strong in New York.   The first has reached its 120th performance.   The second has had about 80.

.   .   .   .   .

J. G.

[*To M. E. R.*]
Chandler
Arizona
March 3 1921

Arizona is a wonderful place for colour and climate. It has done Ada a lot of good. To-morrow we go a motor trip in the mountains for about five days . . . We had a jolly letter from Owen, and his good photo of Biz [their sheep-dog] hung on our shack wall . . . Please thank Ronnie for her note—the bunny-drawings were charming.

All love and blessings

.   .   .

J. G.

[*To M. E. R.*]
Grove Lodge
Hampstead
May 26 1921

Here are three seats for the first matinée of
The First and the Last at the Aldwych on Monday.
I am getting you some also for Thursday evening
at the Comedy.

Hope you'll be able to stand the plays.

. . .

J.

[*To M. E. R.*]
Hotel des Alpes
Madonna Di Campiglio
August 17 1922

We've had a very jolly time.   Three weeks and
more at Cortina, as lovely as ever, but rather too
many noisy Italians.   We motored here from
there by way of Karer See, Bozen, Meran and
Mendel.   Awfully hot in Bozen, but looking lovely,
also Meran.   Mendel spoiled by change of pro-
prietorship in hotel, and Italians generally.   Here
. . . a tennis tournament is in progress, for
which I rashly entered and have won my first
two contests.   In an hour I go forth to be beaten.

This is my first tennis tournament—55, a quaint age to begin such things.

Ada has been very well on the whole and walking splendidly. . . . I have only written one short story out here, and a few pages of another. I do hope . . . that Tom is getting off from London. I am dedicating my new volume of three plays to him: *The Family Man, Loyalties, Windows*. I hope he won't mind.

Cowbells are wonderful here, but cooking pretty poor, though charges are very high. So glad Ronnie is getting some real riding. She ought to make a very good horsewoman with her real fondness for horses . . . bless her.

We leave here on Monday for Milan, via Brescia, and return on August 23 from Milan.

.   .   .   .   .

Your

J.

[*To* M. E. R.]

Grove Lodge
August 26 1922

We're back. A little of the gilt was knocked off by the heat in Milan and the journey home, but on the whole a jolly good time. Ada well, brown, and rather thin. I won my tournament —a cigarette case—much to my surprise.

VERONICA MEREDITH REYNOLDS IN RAGLAN CASTLE
"Ronnie in the Niche"

Those photos you sent . . . were splendid and most original, especially the one with Ronnie in the niche—very strange effects of tone and design.

I shall be rehearsing American *Loyalties* Company until next Friday, then we go back to Wingstone.

.   .   .   .   .

Your

J.

[*To M. E. R.*]

Wingstone

August 30 1923

Just a line to say that I am much better . . . I hope to be out in a few days.

Ada has been a perfect nurse.

.   .   .   .   .

J. G.

[*To M. E. R.*]

Funchal

Madeira

November 21 1923

Ada is distinctly better this last week. This hotel is excellent and the island very pleasant and lovely. Barring our previous arrangements (to go on to Canary Islands) we might have stayed here longer. The climate of course is slack, but very sunny. Our room stands about two hundred feet above the sea with a wide view over it due South.

I have been writing steadily so far. We have not done any excursions, because Ada has not been really fit for motoring in the open. She enjoys the mule-drawn carros, and by walking alongside I get all the exercise I want.

.   .   .   .   .

J.

[*To M. E. R.*
Concerning the play *The Forest*]
Grove Lodge
March 4 1924

Will you and Tom occupy the author's box herewith. I'm cutting back to Biarritz on Thursday morning (keep this dark). Can't bear first nights, and want to get back to her.

Then will you let Dorothy Easton have one of your stalls and Myra [Hess] the other.

I think the play may do all right. There's a wonderful little creature in Hermione Baddeley.

In case I don't see you, all love and blessings. Awful rush

.   .   .

J.

[To M. E. R. from Ada G.]

Merano

November 22 1924

Darling Mabs

. . . Thank you for your lovely birthday messages. We had a quiet day, for I'm still in my room . . .

Jack has been the usual angel he always is in illness. I am more annoyed at my behaviour than I can say in taking up his time in this rotten way, but of course there is no choice about it, and the tiny consolation is that he has a genius for nursing and does really enjoy coffee-making, milk-boiling, and all such games.

We are finding Merano too cold, and it is maddening in a way, for every day the sun shines most gloriously, but does not get into the place till 11, and shoots out of it again at 3. There is a Peruginesque beauty of limpid light before and after sun-time, but not much warmth.

So we plan to trek to Botzen on December 1st, go on to Rome, and then to Palermo, where we hope to stay a month.

Keep us in touch with you, dearest. . . .

.   .   .   .   .

I am

Ever your devoted

Ada

H

[*To M. E. R.*

Referring to certain séances which I attended after our sister's death, notes of which I sent out to him]

Fez

Morocco

March 2 1925

DEAREST MAB

I hasten to answer your letter. . . . Your notes on 'sittings' are of course intensely interesting; but, equally of course, they fit the theory of subconscious mediumistic knowledge (which I take it may be illimitable) just as well as the theory of 'passing over'. But anyway it is truly comforting to know that in the latter case all is well . . .

We are all well, and stay here till Thursday, then we go to . . . Marrakech . . . for two or three weeks; so write there.

.   .   .   .   .

Fez is a strange and wonderful place.

.   .   .   .   .

. . .

J.

J. G. Bound for America, 1925
Sun enough!

[*To M. E. R.*

This reached me in Vienna, where I was working on the translations of several of the books and plays with Herr Leon Schalit, the Austrian translator, to whose staunch and vigorous championship in the early days my brother's work largely owed the start which led to its present popular recognition throughout central Europe. My son joined me, and we went on to Kitzbühel together]

Santa Rita Hotel
Tucson
Arizona

December 9 1925

We are all well, and move on to Chandler, Arizona, on Friday, by way of the Apache trail and Roosevelt Dam. The weather has been curiously unsettled for Arizona, but to-day was most beautiful, and we spent it motoring to the lonely ranch of our old friend Bill Huggett. Everybody here at Tucson has been embarrassingly kind, and we have had rather a hectic time—too hectic for work. Rudy and I have had some good tennis and some riding. I have been acquiring the American seat in jumping with some success. I must have been over a hundred jumps. Ronnie must learn it—it's getting universal.

Ada has had a little ruffle up, but it has subsided again (unberufen).

Yes indeed, I quite realise Schalit's devoted work, and am very grateful.

. . . I'm so sorry you've had sunless weather, but expect by now you're at Kitzbühel.

. . .

J.

[*To M. E. R.*]
The San Marcos
Chandler
Arizona
December 27 1925

I've just received your good letter of December 5 with the list of queries, which I've answered and returned to S. Dearest, I'm most grateful for all your revisions. . . . I'm sending this to Kitzbühel, where you will surely be by now . . . I do hope you and Owen are having a really jolly time . . . bless you both.

We're having glorious sunny dry weather, and it's a beautiful country. We leave here for Redlands, California, on January 16, and after a fortnight there go to the Desert Inn, Palm Springs, California—inland on the edge of the desert, which they say is even drier and warmer than here. There we shall stay six weeks to two months, then go East by way of the Grand Canyon and Santa Fé to Cincinnati and New York, and sail for home on the *Aquitania* on the 16th of

J. G. AND A. G.
In Arizona, 1926

April. I haven't done much work except revision and an address. But I hope to turn out something in the way of a story before getting back.

 . . . . . .

             . . .

               J.

[*To M. E. R.*]
        Grove Lodge
        April 23 1926

Bless you . . . I really am most awfully grateful to you for the work done on the *Saga* and *The White Monkey*! and I tell you what I think would be of immense value to *The Silver Spoon* and its sequel (if I ever write it): If you would go through the English proofs and supply correct English equivalents of the many colloquial and slang expressions with which they are starred, *before* translations are begun. That would really ensure that no important or ridiculous mistakes were made, and would save me the trouble of answering frequent queries. This would be hard and perhaps dull work for you, but it would be (in the circumstances) the most useful.

 . . . Bless you again. It will be jolly to see you all on Tuesday. I will let you have the *Silver Spoon* proofs as soon as I get them.

             . . .

               J.

[*To M. E. R.*]
Union-Castle Line
R.M.S. *Windsor Castle*
December 6 1926

A line to tell you that all goes well with us. Ada quiet in her cabin so far, but not feeling ill. Vi had a bad twelve hours, but is all right again. The boat's a good steady one and the weather moderate. Tomorrow we should run into something warmer and calmer. As usual the utter laziness of ship life has sunk into one's bones. One does nothing except read 'bloods' and toddle about. After Madeira perhaps one may get some order into existence.

Queer rather that ships now take nearly two days longer to the Cape than I took coming back in 1893. We did a record passage of fifteen and a half days in the old *Scot* of 7,000 tons.

I do hope you'll enjoy your Xmas at Bury and have fine weather for it. A fine day there makes an enormous difference. I've secured the old cottage opposite for £—.

.   .   .   .   .

. . .

J.

[*To M. E. R.*]

Queen's Hotel
Sea Point
Cape Town
December 23 1926

We arrived all well on Monday, and are well
and agreeably housed here for some weeks. Rudo
and I both started to work to-day, and it looks
as if the place would be good for us both. It's
on the West (Atlantic) coast about three miles
from Cape Town—a very good hotel. We have
been for three long drives and already seen most
of the country around.   Very beautiful it is—
especially Constantia, Wynberg, etc. Ada stood
the voyage very well for her; and is bobbish so
far . . . The weather is gorgeously sunny, and
here—fortunately—very fresh from the sea breeze.
Many of the places on False Bay (the other side)
would be quite impossible from heat and crowd.
Today we went to Groot Schuur—Rhodes's old
house—now used (like Chequers in England) for
the lodgment of Prime Ministers. It's amazingly
placed for beauty and is a very fine Dutch building (rather heavy interior) with a lovely garden.
But I expect you remember it. Doubt if we shall
go about much. At present we think of staying
here till January 26, then going to Hermanus and
the George District for a fortnight—then up to
the Drakensberg on the borders of Natal, and

back here for a fortnight before sailing for home by the same ship . . .

The flowers are wonderful. The old Dutch farm where I stayed at High Constantia in 1893 has been demolished, and a modern building stands in its place—alack!

Everybody's very kind, but we're avoiding all functions and invitations. Today we just missed seeing a troop of baboons—on the road—coming back from Groot Schuur—bad luck!

.   .   .   .   .

. . .

J.

[*To M. E. R.*]

Bury House
nr. Pulborough
Sussex
August 19 1927

. . . Yes, I had Ronnie's letter. Give her my love and thank her. I'm so glad she has this job; she ought to enjoy it. [Teaching children to ride.] Tell her from me to be very gentle in her methods of instruction. Few youngsters have her nerves, and they want very gentle handling with horses.

.   .   .   .   .

. . .

J.

J. G.

1927

[Photo by Elliott & Fry]

[To his niece Muriel Galsworthy, who wrote asking him to address some small 'Cubs' (Scouts) on kindness to animals]

Grove Lodge
The Grove Hampstead
London N.W.3

Sep. 9 1927

DEAREST MURIEL

Alas, to speak to the very young is beyond me. I shouldn't know what to say. So you must forgive me, my dear, for not being able.

I hope we shall see you at Bury in October.

Our love to you all.

J. G.

[*To M. E. R.*]

Bury House
March 20 1928

So very many thanks, dear, for the . . . glossary, which I return.

Z[1] seems rather to shy at *Fraternity!* They are so chickeny in Austria and Hungary of being tarred with sympathy with the 'Shadows'. They

---

[1] My brother's enthusiastic Viennese publisher, Paul V. Zsolnay, who never spared either pains or expense in producing his finely-printed, attractive editions of J. G.'s translated works.

seem to think that if you shew or feel that, you must be a 'red'. Politics are very downright and crude in those parts.

．　　．　　．　　．　　．

．　．　．

J.

[*To M. E. R.*]

The Birnam Hotel
Dunkeld
Perthshire
August 17 1928

Thank you so very much for your dear letter and the photos. You couldn't have given me anything more precious than a new one of the Dad.

We were very interested to hear your impressions of *Loyalties*, which coincide more or less with mine . . . The houses are extremely good, judging from the nightly returns, so that I hope the play will have another run.

We are enjoying the colour and scents up here . . .

We go on to Inverness and then motor to the foot of Loch Lomond, whence to the Lakes by train, make a day's round there, and then with our own car drive from Shrewsbury to Stanway (Barrie's) and back to Grove Lodge.

．　　．　　．　　．　　．

J.

J. G.'s Godson
Owen Blair Reynolds

[*To M. E. R.*]
Bury House
May 11 1929

We had our first match yesterday—Married v. Single. The Singles had it.

For Married, Rudo 8 and 12
Myself 2   ,,   8 not out.

For the Singles, young Hubert, who came over, 19. It was good fun.

I hope your youngsters will return sound and safe on Friday. I will send Owen a cheque then.

I think the picture [Owen's painting of the Viaduct at Constantine, Algeria] has a lot of poetry in it, and stands out well from the pictures round it [at the R.A.].

. . .

J.

[*To H. Granville Barker*]
Bury House
Sussex
October 5 1930

MY DEAR HARLEY

.   .   .   .   .

The R.S.P.C.A. seem to think that rats and mice are not protected by Law at all, but I'm not sure about this—"needless suffering" covers a lot, even with vermin. My trouble is that I've no experience of that stuff, and I dread experimenting to see for myself; the usual impasse. Perhaps I'll see a way out.

.   .   .   .   .

Always yours

J. G.

[*To M. E. R.*]

Bury House
November 26 1930

DEAREST MAB

So many thanks for the glossary and . . . . . . I'm glad you like Dinny. I'm afraid she's about the only justification for the book; but I have more and more the feeling that novels are no good except for the creation of a character now and then who stays by you.

.   .   .

J.

[*To M. E. R.*

After his horse-accident]

Bury House

December 10 1930

.   .   .   .   .

Thank you for your sweet letters. I am all right except for a healed scar underneath the chin. The doctor took out the stitches today—three days before he originally said. On the whole a very lucky issue. It might have been much worse . . .

It *is* a long time to be away, and I wish it weren't. And I wish—how I wish—we were leaving you really well again. My fervent wishes for your complete restoration, dearest.

Our simplest address will be c/o Charles Scribners . . . New York City . . .

Bless you ever so

.   .   .   .   .

. . .

J.

[*To M. E. R.*]

El Conquistador Hotel
Tucson
Arizona
February 8 1931

I've been most remiss in not writing, but day after day falls into the same routine (most of which is concerned with pen or pencil in hand) and so I've written practically no letters. We're all well. 'The children' away up a cañon for two days (Rudey wants a certain subject). Weather . . . as a rule splendid. Ada is active; walks five or six miles with Vi in the mornings, and in the afternoons runs after our tennis balls, bless her! She and Vi literally do ball-girls for us. Five days a week, R., Vi and I ride at 7.30–8.30. I have a charming little mount. At 9.30 I settle down to the novel and keep it going till nearly lunch time. If only I can keep this up I hope to bring back half the sequel to *Maid in Waiting*. After lunch we lie up a bit, and I tinker at Carmen libretto or read. Tennis for an hour. A grape-fruit. Then more Carmen libretto (finished in the rough, and now being smoothed) till dinner, and after dinner again, while Ada and R. play chess and Vi reads.

The hotel (which is very good) is filling up now; but in our little bungalow we have all the privacy we want, and we've managed to avoid Press and residents. On the 25th February, R.

and V. go to San Francisco and start his exhibition; and A. and I go to the San Marcos Hotel at Chandler, our old haunt, for three weeks.   Thence to San Francisco to start my lecturing tour (8 lectures).   We shall reach New York on April 3, and sail home on April 15.

We do hope the improvement has maintained itself, darling.

·   ·   ·   ·   ·

Your

J.

[*To Denis Mackail*]

Grove Lodge
The Grove
Hampstead N.W.3
November 20 1931

MY DEAR DENIS

What a charming letter! I'm glad you feel like that.   I have reached the age when I'm no use to a critic—*vieux jeu*.   Not, by the way, that I read them.   I emulate the ostrich, and have since 1915.   You will come to that in time, if you haven't already.

·   ·   ·   ·   ·

Always yours

J. G.

Please abbreviate me.

[*To Leon M. Lion*]

> Grove Lodge
> *September* 29 1932

MY DEAR LEON

Our best wishes to you all tonight. We hope to see it on Wednesday next, if you can spare us a box.

By the way, I think:

John Galsworthy O.M.

is a mistake in your advertisements. D.D. (dog's dinner) would have been better, but no letters at all would have been best. May they be suppressed, please?

·   ·   ·   ·   ·

> Yours
> J. G.

John Galsworthy

1928

[*Photo by Pearl Freeman*]